The Practical Guide to Luciferian Witchcraft

Kelly Dawn

Disclaimer

The information provided in this book is not intended as a substitute for professional advice. The author and publisher disclaim any liability, loss, or risk incurred as a consequence, directly or indirectly, of the use and application of any of the contents of this book.

Occult practices and rituals, if explored, should be approached with caution and discretion. Individuals are urged to exercise their own judgment and seek professional advice if needed before engaging in any occult activities.

The author and publisher are not responsible for any consequences resulting from the reader's actions based on the information provided in this book.

Readers are advised that occult practices and beliefs vary widely and may be subject to interpretation. The author does not endorse or promote any specific belief system, and readers are encouraged to explore and question with an open mind.

This book is for readers of age 18 or older.

By reading this book, you acknowledge that you have read and understood this disclaimer. If you do not agree with the terms and conditions outlined herein, you should not proceed to read or engage with the content of this book.

Acknowledgements

Even as solitary practitioners, we're never truly alone on this path.

Stephanie Connolly, thank you for sharing your wisdom and paving the way for other Demonolaters.

Kevin Pappan, thank you for introducing me to the crooked path.

Taylor Ellwood, thank you for your videos; they played a significant role in helping me overcome my fear of working with the demonic.

Adam Knox, thank you for seeing me for what I am before I could.

Table of Contents

Introduction

My aim with this book is to share the insights I've gained while working with Lucifer and the demonic, and to present a practice that you can tailor to suit your personal style.

While the book contains proven manifestation techniques and exercises to guide you in your spiritual growth, the information about who Lucifer and the demonic entities are has emerged from my personal experiences with them, and is not considered the ultimate truth.

Yes, these entities have unique signatures and have been known over the ages for helping humanity in specific areas of life, but to attempt to fully grasp who they are in their entirety would be doing a disservice to the spirits.

When working with the demonic, we're connecting with divine intelligences that exist beyond our scope of human understanding. It's my belief that they will reveal themselves to us in ways that we can understand given where we are on our personal spiritual journey.

Please take what I share in the following pages and use it as a starting point to develop your own relationship with the demonic, discovering who they are for you.

The truth about their nature will be revealed to you through study, practice, and an openness to delve into the depths they will take you to.

Ready?
Let us begin.

Chapter 1: My Journey with Witchcraft

My fascination with the occult took root before I even entered school. Like many children, I was drawn to movies and TV shows featuring witches and wizards, developing a love for anything related to magick, hidden realms, and the mystical.

When I was around the age of 6, my family lived in a turn-of-the-century farmhouse that, despite significant renovations, retained its charm and "oldness." Lights would flicker, doors would open and close on their own, and I reveled in the idea that our house might be haunted, providing me with ghosts to play with.

During our time in that house, one night, my mom and her girlfriends got together to use a Ouija board in an attempt to communicate with any spirits present. To our surprise, they made contact with a spirit named Jesse, who, according to the Ouija board, had lived in the house in the late 1800s and had taken up residence in a toad living in the basement.

The accuracy of this information remains unknown to me. However, what I do know is that I was thrilled with the idea of our house having its very own ghost. A flame of curiosity for the spirit realm was ignited within me, and it would continue to burn for decades to come.

A few years later, I began crafting my own spirit boards, crudely drawing the alphabet on plain white paper and using a mood ring as a planchette. Though I connected with various spirits over the years, my interactions were more like conversations with imaginary friends than formal workings.

In grade 4, my babysitter and I used a board and made contact with the spirit of a young girl. Asking about her death, she revealed she had died in a car accident a few years prior in the city where I lived. Intrigued, my babysitter and I validated her story by researching old newspaper articles in the local library. It was then that I realized, this stuff is REAL.

As I grew older, my interest in spirituality and religion deepened, always seeking a strong connection to the unseen world around me. In my early teens and again in my early 20s, I entertained the idea of becoming a Catholic nun, thinking that spending all day with God would be the ideal way to live.

However, I struggled to reconcile with church dogma, and my experiences with Christianity, while deep and intense over the years, were also brief. I invariably found myself returning to the occult and witchcraft, as that spiritual path felt like 'home.'

My next adventure into the occult world was when I found a giant book on divination at the local mall bookstore that included information on Tarot, Astrology, Palmistry, Numerology, and divination with playing cards.

It felt like I had won the lottery!

I clung to that book and carried it everywhere, filling its pages with numerous notes and highlighting large sections with my pink and yellow markers. My focus was particularly drawn to palmistry, which became my primary interest during that period.

Not long after, I stumbled upon Secrets of Gypsy Fortune Telling by Raymond Buckland, that I studied for hours beneath my favorite tree in the backyard, delving into the divination methods outlined in the book.

My journey continued with Cunningham's The Truth About Witchcraft Today, where the first part of the book explored magick, and the second delved into Wicca. This marked my first encounter with the concept of witchcraft as a religion.

Discovering that Wiccans honored both a god and a goddess, and worked in harmony with nature and the seasons, captivated me. I eagerly sought out as much information as I could.

This was the early '90s, an era before the internet became widespread, but fortunately, witchcraft was undergoing a surge in popularity, and new books were hitting the shelves at the mall.

Influential authors like Laurie Cabot and Silver Ravenwolf led the way, emphasizing the benevolent nature of witchcraft.

They stressed that modern witches rejected any association with the Devil and frowned upon sinister or 'black magick.'

For years, I embraced this 'white light' style of witchcraft and Wicca, blending different elements to create a personal practice that felt authentic to me.

Until 2016, my focus in practice revolved heavily around basic spellwork, working with nature spirits, mastering energy manipulation, and honing my divination skills. During that year, I found myself drawn to exploring the realm of demons and aspects of witchcraft I had previously avoided due to fear.

My interest grew as I delved into occult podcasts, dedicating a few hours each day to tuning into my favorite shows while walking my dog.

It's interesting how, when the spirits seek our attention, they find a way to captivate it.

The topic of demons began surfacing frequently in the regular podcasts I followed. Initially I was hesitant to engage with these episodes because I had been ingrained with the belief, both from my time in church and from witchcraft literature, that demons were inherently evil and to be avoided at all costs.

Curiosity eventually prevailed. I immersed myself in podcast interviews featuring witches and occultists sharing their personal experiences with the demonic, and binge-read books on the topic. The more I discovered positive encounters others had with demons, the more I felt compelled to explore the realm myself.

My first interaction with the demonic was with Morax. After researching different demons, it seemed that he was a friendly and approachable spirit, known for assisting people with natural magick and working with herbs and stones. I decided to summon Morax using a simple ritual with his sigil. However, when contact was established, I was absolutely terrified.

Despite intellectually knowing that demons weren't inherently evil by this point, the deep-seated fear accumulated over the years from religious teachings and Hollywood movies still surfaced. Nevertheless, determined to move forward and connect with the demon, I set aside my fear and continued the encounter.

Uncertain of what to anticipate during the experience, questions swirled in my mind. Would the demon manifest in a physical form? Would I hear his voice? While it wasn't at all like the movies, I distinctly sensed a presence in the room, and my body went ice-cold.

Summoning the courage, I asked Morax if he wanted to form a relationship and work together. Feeling an intuitive 'yes' within, I double-checked with my pendulum, receiving a clear signal to proceed. It seemed the spirit was eager to establish a connection and move forward.

Seeking insights into magick, I offered a drop of blood, and Morax requested the unique exchange of allowing him to experience love through me. My initial reaction was disbelief – a demon desiring love in return for assistance? Seemed pretty strange to me. However, I decided to honor this agreement and spent the subsequent weeks working closely with him.

To fulfill my end of the deal, I consciously chose to replace judgment or anger with love every time those emotions arose. Despite my initial skepticism, the experience turned out to be precisely what I needed for my personal healing, a pattern I've since recognized in my interactions with these spirits over the years. Although we may approach them seeking one thing, they often reveal what we truly need for our growth.

Following this initial encounter, I became more comfortable with the idea of working with the demonic and was committed to further exploring their realm.

Then one day, Lucifer came calling.

Even though I'd moved through a lot of the fear I had associated with working with demons, when the invitation came, my immediate response was a firm 'hell no.' Despite decades of practicing witchcraft, I felt like a novice when it came to engaging with the spirits of the Underworld. I decided to stick with working with other demons, planning to progress to contacting Lucifer when I felt more prepared.

I find it amusing as I write this because one lesson I've learned about the spirit realm is that when they want to work with you, they make it unmistakable, and their persistence is unmatched if they truly desire a connection.

Lucifer started appearing in my awareness constantly, from podcasts to YouTube videos and movies. It felt like I could sense intuitive nudges to work with him, but I was still hesitant.

Eventually, I decided to connect with him, envisioning it as a special event. After all, I planned to invite the Prince of Hell into my home, and I wanted everything to be perfect. I intended to spend time practicing his demonic enn, have his sigil drawn up nicely, get some fresh flowers for an offering, and get the other elements of the working in place before making contact.

However, things didn't unfold as planned. Lucifer had different intentions.

Early on the morning of November 16th, 2016, I headed to Harris Park to play a game of frisbee with my dog Oliver.

To paint the picture, Harris Park (in London, Ontario) is a vast open field lined on one side by the Thames River, and on the other, a small forested area. It was one of our preferred spots for frisbee because there were lights along the river, perfect for our pre-dawn walks, and the huge open field was ideal for Oliver's workout.

That morning, in that park, Lucifer made it clear that it was time to start our working relationship.

If you've ever communicated with a spirit, you understand that their communication differs from human interaction. There's a deeper knowing, beyond words, felt in the body.

I knew this wasn't my imagination. Lucifer was ready to connect.

Initially, I hesitated, not only due to my aforementioned fear of working with Lucifer but also because I wanted to conduct things in the proper manner. I aimed to make contact in my ritual space at home, complete with the correct incense, candles, and his sigil.

It was on that day that I learned spirits aren't overly concerned with such details. Those elements are more for our benefit, helping us attune to the right frequency to establish contact with them. Setting aside my hesitation, I opened myself up to the communication.

As I walked across the park, I could feel energy gathering beneath my feet. This power surged up from the ground and radiated through my entire body. The following words started flowing through me as a chant and didn't even feel as if they were my own.

"Lucifer, fill me with your power,
Your knowledge,
And your wisdom."

Feeling somewhat ridiculous, like a character from a '90s witchcraft movie, I chanted this aloud as I walked across the field. With every step, I sensed more of Lucifer's energy coursing through me.

Upon reaching the other end of the park, I felt the connection fade, signaling the end of our initial meeting. However, the energy lingered as we made our way back home.

During our walk home through downtown, we passed by one of my favorite buildings in the city: the London Life Insurance building. As we walked past it, all of the exterior lights on the side of the building that faced us turned on.

Normally, the building was lit with a few security lights, but that morning, bright, white lights illuminated it like I'd never seen before. Some might dismiss this as a coincidence; however, considering that Oliver and I were regularly out at that time of morning and often played frisbee in the park adjacent to the London Life building, it struck me as significant.

I had never seen the building lit up like that before, and in the years following, never did again.

I took it as a sign.

Lucifer, the Light Bearer, was giving me a little wink.

During the years that followed, I've continued to work with Lucifer and the demonic, and my witchcraft practice has been heavily focused on this type of spirt work.

In the upcoming pages of this book, I'll provide a detailed breakdown of how I connect with these entities and work with them. I'll also present various exercises designed to enhance your psychic abilities and fortify your energetic body.

Additionally, you'll discover techniques for manifesting your will with the assistance of the demonic. Throughout, I'll offer insights and share channeled messages I've received from these entities, providing you with a richer understanding of how they have revealed themselves to me.

As mentioned at the book's outset, I'm sharing my personal experiences, filtered by the lens through which I perceive the world. Recognizing that it's not the ultimate truth but rather my truth based on personal gnosis, I encourage you to embark on your exploration.

Use the practices I share and draw insights from your own encounters with Lucifer and the demonic to discern what holds true for you.

Chapter 2: Who Is Lucifer?

Lucifer is one of those entities shrouded in mystery, and over the years of trying to figure out exactly who he is, I've come to this conclusion:

It really depends on how you choose to see him. He wears different masks based on how the practitioner needs to experience him.

To some, he appears as a fallen angel expelled from the heavens for refusing to conform to the same tune as others.

To others, he embodies the role of the Light Bearer, serving as a guide to lift the veil that has obscured humanity's understanding, allowing us to grasp the extent of our power.

For another set, he represents rebellion, challenging the established norms and questioning our accepted truths, urging individuals to explore their own understanding.

Finally, there are those who perceive him as the Devil himself—the trickster and Lord of Lies reigning over the earth, enticing humanity to indulge in sinful behavior.

I asked AI, which some believe was developed with the help of Lucifer himself, how Lucifer is viewed from different perspectives, and here's what it shared:

Morning Star: In Latin, "Lucifer" means "light-bringer" or "morning star." Originally, it referred to the planet Venus when it appears in the east before sunrise. In this sense, Lucifer symbolizes the dawning of light and knowledge.

Satanic Interpretation: In some branches of modern Satanism, Lucifer is considered a symbol of personal enlightenment, individualism, and rebellion against religious dogma and authority. This interpretation often views Lucifer as a liberating figure who encourages self-discovery and defiance against oppressive systems.

Fallen Angel: The most common association with Lucifer comes from Christian theology. According to the Christian tradition, Lucifer was an angel who rebelled against God and was cast out of Heaven, becoming Satan or the Devil. This interpretation depicts Lucifer as a symbol of pride, rebellion, and temptation.

Hermetic and Occult Traditions: In various occult and esoteric traditions, Lucifer may represent the light of intellect, inner illumination, and spiritual enlightenment. Some occultists view Lucifer as a metaphor for the quest for knowledge and self-discovery. It's important to note that these interpretations often distance Lucifer from the Christian devil and emphasize a more nuanced understanding.

Prometheus Archetype: In some esoteric circles, Lucifer is equated with the archetype of Prometheus, who brought fire (knowledge) to humanity. In this context, Lucifer is seen as a symbol of enlightenment, innovation, and the pursuit of wisdom. *(ChatGPT, 2023)*

Over the course of my relationship with Lucifer, he's appeared as all of these at different times.

Sometimes he comes to help us embody our inner adversary and question what we've believed to be normal, or as the Light Bringer here to shed light on the aspects within ourselves that we'd rather not look at, and at other times, he comes to us as the mischievous devil to help us connect with our rebellious, pleasure-seeking side.

He can come across as harsh, but only because he sees our potential and holds us to a high standard. Regardless of how he has appeared to me over the years, the main messages I have received from him are about the importance of humanity coming back to the remembrance that we are powerful creators and that we need to take responsibility for our lives and what we make of them.

During meditation, I asked Lucifer about his role with humanity and how he and the demonic help us. Below is the channeled message that came through:

"I am here to liberate and set you free from the confines of your mind and limited understanding.

The power at your command is incomprehensible to you. For how are we to put into words that the same power that creates worlds dwells within you, ready to be activated and utilized whenever you desire.

I am here to illuminate and show you aspects of yourself that you've kept hidden from view, whether consciously or not. When you bring these into the light, they can be examined, transmuted, and integrated to serve you better.

It's when you see all parts of yourself and know that you possess within you everything that is good and evil, everything that is of the darkness and of the light that you rise in power because others can't hold who you are against you any longer.

I am here to help you see the beauty of this earthly life and to help you enjoy the rich pleasures that are available to you.

You were given these human bodies with their thirst for worldly things because you were meant to enjoy them. Along with this, though, has to come the deep wisdom that it's not those things that are the treasures.

Many have accumulated material things and have had the experiences they lusted after only to find them meaningless and empty.

How beautiful is that for then the wise are driven toward a deeper understanding of who they are as spiritual beings, while the foolish continue on their quest choosing to feed on things that only leave them yearning for more, contributing to their emptiness.

I am here to ignite the black flame that dwells within you so you can awaken to the truth that there's more to this world than meets the eye, and to help you better understand your purpose and mission. When you're guided by this flame, you're pulled deeper into your greatness.

You hunger for change within yourself because you know that is the only real thing in your control, and through this control of the beast within, utilizing your divine power, you are able to do great things.

I am here to light the way for you as you journey through your human experience, showing you signs that lead you in the direction that will bring you back to remembrance of who you are and what you're capable of.

While this path isn't easy to walk, when you allow yourself to be guided by the dark flame within, you will access the deepest parts of yourself and unlock the mysteries of this life you've chosen to participate in."

Who will Lucifer be for you?

Which aspect will he manifest as for you?

Those answers will be revealed through meditation and spirit connection, which we'll discuss in the following chapters.

Chapter 3: The Nature of the Demonic

When most people encounter the term "demon", their thoughts often veer toward terrifying hellish beings on a mission to torment and destroy humanity.

This perception can be traced back to monotheistic religions such as Christianity. As this religion spread across nations, individuals faced a stark choice: either renounce their worship of pagan gods and goddesses or confront dire consequences.

Over time, the deities from cultures influenced by monotheism were driven underground, both metaphorically and literally, and were cast as malevolent forces to be feared and avoided at all costs. Anything not associated with the monotheistic god or approved by him was deemed Satanic.

Hollywood further contributes to the fear associated with these entities. According to most movies and TV shows, demons are portrayed as the antagonists, spirits that must be fought against and banished to the Underworld for peace to reign on earth.

The notion that demons are hell-bent on destroying humanity is ridiculous. Blaming actions on demons often serves as a means for people to avoid taking personal responsibility for their human nature, which, let's be honest, isn't always pleasant.

Humans possess the capacity to commit horrific acts, and attributing these actions to the devil or demons becomes a way to excuse vile behavior.

Another reason people shy away from working with demons stems from the experiences of other magickal practitioners. When witches have negative encounters with demons, it typically falls into one of two categories: they are either harboring a lot of fear, attracting entities of a similar vibration, or they are being disrespectful to the spirit.

Not everything in the spirit realm wants to help us. Just as there are parasitic humans causing chaos in the lives of others, there are entities doing the same. Opening up to the spirit realm draws attention from various spirits, not solely the demons one intends to connect with.

Issues also arise with demons when practitioners are disrespectful and resort to threats if the spirits do not comply with their demands. Demonic entities are not to be seen as above us, and as practitioners of the Left Hand Path, we don't bow down groveling before them. However, we treat them with respect.

This respect is similar to how we treat fire or electricity. With the demonic, we're working with powerful, often primordial entities that have been around longer than we can fathom.

Requesting the presence of the demonic in a respectful manner and expressing gratitude for guidance, assistance, or protection goes a long way.

Does this imply that all demons are inherently loving and benevolent? No. Similar to how death and destruction are inherent aspects of nature, they also exist within the realm of demons.

In our contemporary era, there exists an imbalanced fixation on 'love and light,' with some people considering it the sole valid manifestation of the divine. However, the divine Universe encompasses everything, including our darker aspects and inclinations toward what some label as 'bad'; denying these aspects would be a rejection of our true selves.

We embody the entirety of the Universe within us—the light and the dark, what we categorize as good and bad. Operating on a spectrum, we dance between these diverse ways of being, fully experiencing the consequences that accompany each.

Demons, much like everything else in our Universe, are energy. They are dynamic currents of power that we can tap into. Despite the names and associations we've given them based on our human understanding, these entities fundamentally exist as frequencies.

The confusion often stems from the specific associations made with certain demons.

Consider Pazuzu, for instance, known as a storm demon causing chaos and destruction. While this characterization may hold true, individuals with a working relationship with Pazuzu, seeing him as an energetic force, can invoke him to govern storms, influence the weather, enhance their understanding of weather patterns, or receive advanced notice of storms for better preparation.

When we engage with demons in a respectful way, we form alliances with these energetic currents and natural forces rather than attempting to control or wage war against them.

One of the main reasons people are drawn to working with the demonic is because of their ability to assist us with the very real-world issues we face as humans. These entities are renowned for aiding in basic earthly pleasures—money, sex, and power.

However, by collaborating with Lucifer and demonic entities, we undergo spiritual and personal transformations that propel us into a deeper alignment with our true selves, enabling us to understand that those things we seek externally are created within.

So yes, demons will help us get more money, get laid, and achieve success, but it goes so much deeper than that.

Demons help us navigate through our inner landscape, teaching us about the physical and non-physical worlds, assisting us in seeing our blind spots and doing shadow work, and aiding us in manifesting our will.

A frequently asked question is, 'Which demons should I consider working with?'

I recommend starting your exploration with Lucifer and the demons introduced in this book: Flereous, Leviathon, and Belial because they rule over the elements that we as humans embody: air, fire, water, and earth, and will help you stay energetically balanced in your practice.

It's important to recognize that their specific energy might not immediately resonate with you (although it might in the future), and other demons might be more suitable for you to work with.

Demons guide us to explore the depths of our being, and sometimes, we may not be at the point in our personal growth for certain relationships.

For instance, connecting with Leviathon might be less suitable if you haven't delved into significant inner work with your emotions, given his association with water and its ties to our emotional depths. In this case, it might be more appropriate for you to work with a different demon that is associated with water to keep the elemental energies balanced.

Do your research on various demons and don't try to force relationships with spirits. Those meant for you will reveal themselves when you're prepared. You might receive messages in dreams or experience an inner knowing that a specific demon is calling out to you. Alternatively, they might manifest in your daily life like they did for me through mediums like podcasts, movies, or social media.

If you sense no spirit reaching out to you for contact, you can request a sign from the demonic to initiate a relationship.

This can be as straightforward as stating aloud, **'I'm feeling the call to work with the demonic. If it's for my highest good, I'm open to receiving a sign that it's time to move forward on this path.'**

In spirit communication, there's always a risk of attracting unwanted entities that are not demons but rather parasitic entities or less harmful yet still annoying little nasties.

With magick, like life in general, there are dangers.

Steps you can take to ensure you're protecting yourself:

Practice Preparation: Engage in meditation, energy work to build up your energetic body, and establish your astral workspace before delving into spirit communication.

Set Clear Intentions: Intend that only beings for your highest good will make contact with you. Maintain firm boundaries in your mundane life; just as leaky boundaries can attract people who want to use you, the same can happen with spirits. Clearly define what you're available for, and tolerate nothing less.

Stabilize Your Mental State: Avoid working with spirits when you're overly emotional or struggling with untreated mental health issues. Spirits are drawn to our energy, and being in a stable emotional and mental state is crucial. It's advisable to address these issues through therapy, coaching, medication, or other methods before connecting with entities. If struggling, consider working with Universal energy, your ancestors, or personal spirit guides with whom you already have a working relationship.

Be Respectful: Treat the demonic with the same respect you'd have with another human. While traditional methods of summoning demons might work for some practitioners, the approach of calling them into a triangle and forcing them to comply with your bidding can lead to negative experiences. A healthy connection with the demonic, like any relationship, thrives when neither party is coerced, and there's a mutual desire to work together.

Chapter 4: Channeled Messages from Lucifer and the Demonic

In the upcoming pages, you'll find channeled messages from Lucifer, Flereous, Leviathon, and Belial. These insights are shared to provide you with a glimpse into how these entities have manifested themselves to me through personal gnosis.

I am Lucifer

The Light Bringer

I'm the one who helps you see what you must see in order to manifest your deepest desires

I shine light on your shadow, I illuminate your path and help bring you clarity. I ignite the divine flame of your consciousness so you can carry out your life's greatest work

People have feared me over the years because I represent liberation and enlightenment

For if people understood their power to create at will whatever they desire, the world would be a very different place

A better place

And the slave god would lose his power

Now some people reading this might worry what people would do with that power

Would they go mad with it and use it for evil? The answer is some would, yes, but it's not like they don't do that already

Right now, this is happening in mass amounts because of the slave system that's in place

People feel powerless

They feel the need to control others because they don't feel like they have any control over their reality

But if they did know that, if they knew what I teach, they wouldn't feel the need to have power over others because it wouldn't serve them

They would understand that they, as consciousness, hold the ability to manifest whatever they want so why bother with any of the nonsense you see today

I'm here to liberate

To bring freedom to those who feel the need to rebel against the system that is so clearly broken, so they can return to their seat on the throne of power that all of you get to reign from

For you each have your own kingdom which is your own life, and you get to manifest into that kingdom whatever you choose

I am Flereous

The one who stirs up your wildest passion for your life's adventure

I help you burn through the illusions that do not serve you so you can reveal who you truly are at your core

I fuel your greatest passion for creation and feed you when you need to rise to the occasion

For your creative vision needs fuel. It can't just be fed with the mind but with the heat that arises when you connect with your heart

I am the one they call on when there is stagnation and old things need to fall away

I am the force within you that you call upon when you feel like you don't have the strength

I am the power that mothers find when they need to lift a car off their child in order to save them

I'm here to be a source of power when you find yourself feeling weak, a source of inspiration when your mind has grown dull, and a refuge for those who require the inner strength to do what they don't feel they can do on their own

I am Leviathon

The great beast of the sea who rules over emotions and helps you either stir them up or regulate them depending on your needs and desires

It is I who helps you connect to the deepest parts of yourself

The parts that have long lain dormant because you fear what would be unleashed if you allowed yourself to feel them

I am the one who helps you embrace your wildness, your darkness, and the parts of yourself that will not be tamed

As the great dragon, I help you ride the waves of your emotions so they no longer have power over you

I am the one they call on when the pain of life becomes so great it feels like you're drowning in sorrow

I am the one who finds you at your lowest point, sinking into the pits of despair and helps you rise up so you can carry out the work you're here to do

Call on me when you feel disconnected from your emotions

Call on me when you need to traverse your inner world, not with the mind, but with your inner knowing

I am the gatekeeper to the great Abyss where you'll learn the secrets of the unknown

Together we ride out the storms as I help you balance the emotional turbulence you encounter within

I am Belial

Demon that rules over all that helps you feel stable in your humanness

I am the rock that you can lean on when life feels tumultuous for I am steady

I am the one who helps you create form and put the ideas of your mind and the feelings of your heart into grounded action

Call on me when you need to take practical action

When you can't muster up the strength and order to carry out the steps you know you need to take in order to manifest the deepest desires of your soul

For it is I who helps you bring what is unseen into the physical realm where you can see the evidence of the inner work you've done

When you need grounding, when you need to feel like you are one with this earth, I am the one who loves your humanness

Your body in all its fleshy beauty can only function at its best when you're firmly rooted into your reality with action

For you were not created to spend all day just thinking about things

You were given a human body to move, to create with your hands the ideas your consciousness dropped into your mind and heart

Call on me when you need to feel connected to this realm

When you'd rather escape your humanity through the numbing of drugs, tv, or habits that dissociate you

Call on me when you need to put your great plans into action for I am the one who stabilizes that which is within you so you can bring it into physical form

Message from Lucifer when asked about the role of magick in our lives:

Magick is your birthright

A natural way of being and interacting with the world

It's something the false god has tried to keep from you

Shame you for using it to lure you away from the truth of who you are

For can you imagine a whole world filled with people creating what they want?

Knowing that they hold that power and therefore no longer have to fight, struggle, and harm others for what they think they're lacking?

With that kind of unity comes massive amounts of power and the false god and his warriors won't have that

It's too threatening to their system

But more and more are waking up to the truth that magick is real and a way to interact with your world to create the change you wish to see

How you go about doing magick is up to you, for there are many systems out there you can choose from

None are wrong, and all are valid

The basic process for any magick you do is simple

Ask yourself what you want

Do the workings to create that change

Believe with every cell in your being that it is so

And pay attention to ways you can help birth those desires into your reality

We (myself and other entities) are always here to help you, but the manifestation of your desires is always a result of the changes that occur within you

We can pave the way to make the process easier

We can show you what you must see within yourself and we can guide you to your next best steps, but it really all comes down to you and what you're choosing

Look for the evidence

Magick is all around you

Found in your so-called miracles

Look to nature

See the way the world outside of your humanness works, and you'll see magick in motion every day

You like to complicate things

In love with the suffering, which is something that's been ingrained in you since the false god chose to enslave you

That's why so many of you struggle and stay stuck

The addiction to suffering

But it's not even real

The chains must be broken and the enslaved set free

That's what I'm (we) are here to do

Knowledge, wisdom, and power

That which you seek through us is already within you, and we're here to be a mirror of that

To remind

To awaken

To set free

We come to you with different faces so that you may each understand this in your way

Each demon is programmed with the codes to your growth and enlightenment

Whether you label them positive or negative, they're each here to show you what you must see

Through magick

Through ritual and connection

You gain the understanding we're here to give you

43

Message from Lucifer about embracing all aspects of self

Those who refuse to dance with their own darkness will be consumed by it

For the avoidance of what you label as the wickedness within only allows it to fester and grow

When you embrace all parts of who you are

Acknowledging what makes you both human and divine

You bring yourself back into wholeness

For when you no longer feel the need to hide from the truth of what you are
You release the chains that have kept you bound by limitation

You are the sun and the moon
The storm and the calm
The sea and the desert
The joy and the agony

You are the ALL that is

Chapter 5: Setting Up Your Altar

The first thing you'll want to do when getting started on this path is to create sacred space in your home and set up an altar. This space need not be extensive, and your altar can range from simple to elaborate.

The main purpose is to create an inviting space for Lucifer and the demonic to be present, to cultivate an energetic vortex in your home that's a potent area to do magick, and that acts as a space between the realms for your spiritual work.

This doesn't mean that the spirits aren't with you when you're away from home. You can interact with them outdoors or while traveling, but having a sacred space in your home sets up a powerful working area.

For a witch, having a dedicated magickal space in the home is akin to an artist having their studio or a chef having a kitchen tailored to their liking.

This space serves as a power hub and acts as a cue to your mind that you're about to engage in an activity that transcends your ordinary life, shifting your focus from the tangible to the mystical realm where access to other worlds becomes easier.

Our homes are living entities that safeguard us and provide a backdrop for the realization of our dreams and desires. By infusing this space with the energy of the demonic through sacred arrangements, we create a more harmonious living environment.

The four main demons discussed in this book are associated with the elements: Lucifer with Air, Flereous with Fire, Leviathon with Water, and Belial with Earth.

When we consciously connect with the elements, we, in turn, achieve a greater sense of balance because the energy of the elements is infused into who we are.

Being unbalanced in our elemental energy can show up in the following ways:

Air: scattered thinking or being overly rigid in our beliefs

Fire: angry and hot-headed or lacking passion and drive

Water: reacting emotionally to circumstances or being closed off to feelings

Earth: feeling stuck in life and unable to move forward or not grounded enough in reality

Ideally, your altar should face East and can be any size you find suitable. Some people prefer to have a small table set in a corner of their living room, while others have entire temple rooms in their home devoted to magickal work.

It's advisable not to have the altar in your bedroom as it can interfere with sleep patterns and it's best if you are the only one coming into regular contact with it.

Your altar serves as a sacred space infused with both your energy and that of the spirits you engage with. While it's not the end of the world to have other family members or visitors interact with items on your altar, be conscious that energy transfer occurs among the living and spirits. Therefore, exercise caution and be mindful of who you permit into your workspace.

As with everything, adapt when you need to. If you can't set up a permanent altar due to your living arrangements, try to use the same area of your living space for your practice. You can have a few items that you set up when practicing and then store them away safely until it's time to do another magickal working.

The same thing applies if you're traveling. You don't need to pack up all of your tools to take with you, but you could use the same corner of your hotel room to meditate in while you're away.

Below are some items that you might like to have on your altar:

Sigil of Lucifer

Sigils act as gateway connection points to the spirits you want to work with and can be drawn on a piece of paper, carved into wood or clay, or painted on a surface. The sigil of Lucifer on my personal altar is made from a piece of paper from my book of shadows with the sigil drawn in black marker, placed inside a 5x7 picture frame from the dollar store. Simple and effective.

Statue of Baphomet

Baphomet, the Sabbatic Goat, encompasses all that is. This figure represents the masculine and feminine, our animal and divine self, the eternal flame of knowledge, and it represents the spiritual authority we hold as Luciferians over our earthly endeavors.

Elemental Symbols

A connection to the elements of earth, air, fire, and water will ground you in your power and help you feel more balanced as you work your magick.

To represent the elements on your altar, you can use the sigils of Lucifer/Air, Flereous/Fire, Leviathon/Water, Belial/Earth, or use the following items that are common among many witchcraft traditions:

Air: sword or athame
Fire: wand
Water: cup or chalice
Earth: rock or a small dish filled with earth

Working Candle

This is a simple candle in the color of your choosing that you light whenever you're doing any kind of work at your altar, even if it's just meditation. This acts as a signal to your subconscious mind that you're about to embark on sacred work and can be a focus point for meditation, as well as a way to communicate with spirits.

Mine is a plain white pillar candle a few inches in diameter I purchased from the local home decor shop. It's always lit when I'm at the altar, and I've found that spirits love to 'speak' through the flame. It will dance wildly back and forth when they're giving me a 'yes' answer and get so small that it almost disappears into the wax if it's a 'no'.

Sigils of Other Demons

Along with the sigil of Lucifer, you may wish to have the sigils of other demons you work with regularly on your altar. These can be drawn on paper, carved into wood or clay, or painted on other surfaces. When I'm connecting with a demon for a particular working, I'll have their sigil on my altar, and when the working is finished, I'll store it away until future use.

Your Magickal Journal

Your magickal journal can range from a simple notebook from the dollar store to a beautifully bound book with handmade paper depending on your personal taste.

In this journal, you'll write down any notes from your magickal practice and the work you do with the demonic.

To keep things organized, I like to have a separate journal to record my nightly dreams, one for daily mindset work, a simple notebook I use for doodling when channeling spirit messages, and a leather bound Book of Shadows that I use to record the main elements of my practice.

Demonic Sigils

Lucifer

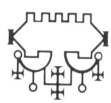

Belial

Leviathon

Flereous

Chapter 6: Creating Your Astral Temple

Whenever we engage in magick and connect with spirits, we operate outside the confines of space and time as we know it.

We delve into the unseen realm, the astral plane, where all of our desires already exist. While there's no actual separation between our regular day-to-day life and the unseen realm, it's helpful to set the intention that we're practicing magick in this space beyond our normal life. This helps free us from self-imposed limitations and detach from beliefs we might be holding that can prevent us from bringing our desires to life.

Most of us carry stories about why we can or can't achieve our goals. In the unseen realm, we can release ourselves from these stories to access the frequency of what we want to manifest more easily.

Below you'll find two variations of the astral temple: one in the Underworld, and one in a garden. Experiment, choose what feels best for you, and then commit to visiting the same temple regularly to build up the energy there.

The Underworld Temple

To create your Underworld temple, sit comfortably in front of your altar, and take a few moments to calm your mind and body with meditation.

With your eyes closed, imagine a comfortable environment—a spot in your favorite forest, a beach, the backyard of your childhood home, or a cozy corner of a coffee shop. If you can't think of any place from your waking life, use a place from a movie or one that comes intuitively.

Next, envision a door appearing in this space. This door can look however you want, made of any materials. Notice its details: material, color, and handle. When you touch the door, how does it feel? When you push or pull, is it heavy or does it glide open effortlessly?

Open the door, revealing stairs descending into the earth with thirteen steps. Like the door, these stairs can be of any material. Walk down, counting from one to thirteen.

Your temple is at the bottom, built with your imagination. This is your workspace in the unseen realm, and it gets to look however you want.

See yourself stepping inside and look around. What does the first room look like? What color are the walls? Is there furniture? Spend time building this image and expand upon it when it feels right for you.

Once you've visualized this space, engage your other senses by noticing its smells, sounds, and textures.

As you become more comfortable in the temple, add more rooms. When I started, mine resembled a living room; over time, I added a library, a boardroom for spirit guide meetings, a magickal working room, and an energy healing room.

Also visualize a separate doorway for your demonic guides and other spirits to enter and exit through.

When you're at the point in your practice to meet with spirits, mentally see these entities passing through a white light before entering and leaving to ensure they're not bringing unwanted energies into your space or taking outside energy back to their realm.

Visit your temple daily, using your senses to make it come alive each time. Note details in your magickal journal, draw pictures, or gather online images.

When leaving, walk back up the thirteen steps and exit through the same door you entered through. Consistent entry and exit through this door will help move you between levels of consciousness safely. If you feel disoriented after visiting your astral temple, have a light snack to ground back into the physical realm.

Magick Garden

Construct this astral temple similarly to the Underworld Temple. Instead of the door leading to a staircase, imagine it opens into a beautiful garden with thirteen stepping stones leading you deeper into the garden.

Follow the thirteen steps and let your imagination fill in the garden's details. Notice the trees, flowers, and ground covering. Are there animals in your garden? Is there a sitting area with benches or tables?

Once you've visualized this space, engage your other senses by noticing its smells, sounds, and textures.

Just like with the other astral temple style, visualize another door in your garden for your spirit guests to enter and exit your astral space.

When leaving your garden, walk back over the thirteen stepping stones, and go out through the same door you entered.

Chapter 7: Meditation

At the core of a solid magickal practice is meditation for two key reasons:

1. It helps you see that you are separate from your thoughts and be more selective with the ones you choose to identify with. Since thoughts and beliefs play a huge role in manifesting, this will help you construct a mindset that will support your goals.

2. It helps you access altered states of consciousness where you're able to connect with multi-dimensional beings more easily and move beyond the limitations of space and time so you can bend and shape your reality easier.

We become very attached to who we think we are and meditation moves us into a place of remembrance that we are far more than just physical bodies. It's through this detachment of the self as we know it that we're able to experience all that we are as spiritual beings.

If you're brand new to meditation, start with 5 minutes at a time and work your way up from there. Ideally, you want to be spending about 20 minutes per day in meditation.

When you're meditating, you're building up your psychic muscle and it will strengthen over time with regular use. A warning for those who love to jump in head first and go hard; if you overdo it with meditation, you'll most likely experience psychic burnout. Just like you wouldn't walk into a gym after not working out for months and try to deadlift 200lbs, don't start doing 2 hours of meditation if you're brand new to the practice, or haven't done it for a while.

The path of witchcraft is never ending and there's no rush to be anywhere you're not ready to be yet.

Basic Meditation

Sit comfortably in front of your altar with your legs crossed or in a chair. If you're sitting on the floor, you can tuck a rolled-up towel, blanket, or cushion under yourself to tilt your body forward a bit and offer your lower back more support. Keep your spine straight, and if you tend to get chilly, wrap a blanket around yourself.

You can also sit with your legs underneath you in a kneeling position if that's more comfortable. I find it's easier to have better posture in this position and use a small, wooden meditation bench to sit on to keep my legs from falling asleep.

To begin, light your working candle and set a timer on your phone for however long you want to meditate for.

Close your eyes and inhale to the count of 4, hold the breath for a count of 4, and exhale for a count of 4.

Throughout the time you're meditating, focus on the breath. When thoughts come into your head, don't try to force your mind to be quiet or still, simply go back to focusing on your breath.

When your timer goes off, record any information in your magickal journal you'd like to keep track of.

You can include the length of time you spent meditating, the time of day, the current moon phase, the current weather, and the overall mood you were in before and after your practice.

You can also include any insights you received during your meditation such as intuitive messages, mental images that came through, changes in temperature, bodily sensations you experienced, or any other information you feel is relevant.

I find spirit likes to speak to me through animal messengers often, so in my own practice, I'll note down if I hear the blue jays, crows, or coyotes around my property being particularly active during my meditation time.

Candle Flame Meditation

As with the basic meditation practice, sit in front of your altar in a comfortable position, set the timer on your phone, and light your working candle.

Gaze softly at the flame with your eyes relaxed. This soft gaze is the same kind you experience when you catch yourself staring out the window daydreaming, or if you've ever looked at one of those Magic Eye pictures that reveal another image when you look at it with relaxed focus.

Breathe deeply and slowly as you gaze into the flame. Don't worry about counting inhales and exhales with this method, but be intentional to breathe from your diaphragm and not your chest.

This meditation is perfect if you're feeling scattered or overwhelmed because as you focus your eyes on the single point of the candle flame, you're signaling to your mind that it's safe to focus as well.

When thoughts arise, gently bring your attention back to the flame and continue breathing.

Record any relevant information in your magickal journal.

Breathing Through The Body

Sit or lie down comfortably in front of your altar with your working candle lit.

Close your eyes, take a few deep breaths, and bring your awareness to your left big toe. Then imagine that you're breathing through your left toe. Imagine air being inhaled through the skin on your toe and being released and exhaled through the skin as well.

Expand the surface area and now imagine breathing through your entire foot. Continue with this process, expanding up to your ankle, calf, knee, upper leg, and then from the right big toe moving up the other leg in the same fashion.

Once you're breathing through both legs, set the intention to breathe through your torso, chest, arms, fingers, and right up to your neck and head.

You're now breathing through every part of your body and you should feel a deep level of relaxation.

You can stay in this meditation, breathing through your body for a few more minutes, or use it as a primer before entering the Void Meditation.

The Void Meditation

This is the meditation I use the most in my personal practice as it moves you deep into the realm of dark matter where it's easier to connect with other beings and with the different possibilities available to manifest in your life.

Sit comfortably in front of your altar with your working candle lit and gaze softly at the flame for a few moments to bring your mind into focus.

Breathe slowly and deeply, inhaling for a count of 4, holding that breath for a count of 4, and exhaling for a count of 4.

Close your eyes and imagine yourself floating in complete darkness.

You are weightless and surrounded by the dark matter of creation. Imagine this infinite sea of darkness in front of you as far as you can, behind you, and on both sides of you.

You are one with this dark matter
One with the Void
One with the energy that creates all that is

Breathe deeply now at the pace your body wants to go, feeling your diaphragm expand as you inhale through your nose and contract as you exhale through your mouth.

Imagine with every inhale, you're breathing in energy from the Void. There is an infinite supply of this energy, and as it moves into your body, it's filling your cells with the creative force of the Universe itself.

As you exhale, imagine any stale, stagnant energy leaving your body through your mouth and immediately being transformed by the Void back into creative energy.

Perform this breathing exercise until it feels like you have cleared the stagnant energy from your body.

Get comfortable practicing this for at least 5 minutes at a time, and then work your way up to 20 minutes.

Meditating with Demonic Enns

Enns are words from an unknown (demonic) language that are used in a similar way that mantras are.

They can be used to connect with the spirits for communication, for protection, or to attune your frequency with particular demons. *For more detailed information on demonic enns, refer to S. Connolly's book, The Complete Book of Demonolatry, 2008.*

For this meditation, start with Lucifer's enn and then move on to using the enns of the other elemental demons once you're comfortable with the process.

To begin, light your working candle and sit comfortably in front of your altar. Have the demonic enn written on a piece of paper for reference as you're chanting it.

Take a few moments to breathe deeply as you softly gaze at the candle flame and then begin chanting Lucifer's enn:

Renich Tasa Uberaca Biasa Icar Lucifer

Continue chanting the enn while in a light meditative state for 5-10 minutes. You can also use prayer beads and recite the enn as your fingers move over each bead.

We'll discuss further communication and connection with Lucifer and the demonic in a later chapter, but this chanting will act a primer getting you used to what their energy feels like.

Below is a list of the enns associated with the other elemental demons. When you feel ready, go through the same meditation process you did with Lucifer above, substituting the other demonic enns.

Flereous - Ganic Tasa Fubin Flereous

Leviathan - Jaden Tasa Hoet Naca Leviathan

Belial - Lirach Tasa Vefa Wehlc Belial

Notice anything that comes up for you during your meditation and make notes in your magickal journal.

Chapter 8: Energy Work

Along with meditation, working with energy consistently creates a strong magickal practice as you're working with the non-physical substance of creation itself.

Everything in our Universe is made of energy, and there's no separation between anything.

The things that appear solid, like the chair you're sitting in, are, in fact, particles in motion that if looked at under a strong enough microscope, wouldn't appear to be solid at all.

Whether we're communicating with spirits or manifesting our will, we're working with the energy that connects all that is, ever has been, and all that ever will be.

This concept came fully to life for me about 10 years ago when I discovered spoon bending.

At that time, I had heard about people being able to bend metal spoons with their mind, but I thought it was something reserved for stage magicians or specially trained energy healers who had spent years perfecting their skills.

Then one day, I was reading a book by life coach Martha Beck, and she talked about her experiences with bending cutlery.

In a split second, a new paradigm opened up to me. This woman wasn't talking about doing parlour tricks, and she wasn't a trained energy worker. She holds degrees from Harvard, is highly recognized in her industry, and is known for being one of the best coaches out there.

My (often overly) analytical, Capricorn brain was paying full attention as she described how she used the power of her mind and a small amount of physical force to bend spoons. I thought, 'If she could do this, maybe I could too.'

I immediately rushed over to my kitchen drawer and pulled out a fork.

I went deep into meditation and entered the Void.

This was the first time I'd accessed that level of consciousness, and at the time, I described it as being in deep space. It felt like I was floating in nothingness, and at the same time, it felt like I had access to everything.

I could feel my third eye buzzing as I allowed myself to go deeper and deeper into the darkness. All the while, I was holding the fork loosely in my hand, being careful not to grip it too tightly because I didn't want to warm up the metal, making it easier to bend with physical force.

When I got the hit from my intuition to begin bending the fork, I held it loosely by one end and started gently bobbing it up and down. I opened my eyes and gazed softly at the fork, seeing it more like a blurry object in motion between different states rather than something purely solid.

As a kid in school, we used to do this with pencils. We'd shake them gently so they appeared to be 'rubber'. I brought this same imagery to the fork-bending exercise.

Then I started to imagine the fork being one with my hand. I mentally zoomed in, and instead of seeing both as separate and solid, I visualized them as a cloud of particles merging with each other and with Universal energy.

I could feel my body shiver and knew I had hit on something important.

I imagined the fork doing what I wanted it to do, seeing it bend and twist around itself with ease. When the moment felt right, I applied a little bit of pressure to the fork.

Nothing happened.

So I repeated the process of bobbing the fork up and down gently and mentally seeing it merge with my hand. When my intuition gave me the nudge, I applied pressure again to the fork, and this time, it felt like something else was moving through me. It was a force and a power that seemed too intense to even be able to put into words, but it could be felt.

The fork became as malleable as a thin paperclip, and with barely any physical force, I twisted it into a nice bend. The ease at which this happened was like cutting through butter with a hot knife.

Seconds later, the fork returned to the form I was most familiar with; solid, hard metal. I once again pushed down on the ends of the fork as if to bend it. It wouldn't budge, and if I were to try to undo the bend that had just been created, I'd need a pair of pliers and have to muscle it back to its original shape.

It was around 5 am when this happened, and I think I waited until 6 am before calling my mom because I had to share this with someone. I wanted to remember this moment forever because I knew something massive had shifted in my perception of reality.

"Mom… I just bent a fork using my mind!!'

'What?!'

And then I shared with her everything that happened so it would feel even more real for me.

When we have experiences that contradict our normal view of reality, it's important to make note of them so our brain can have proof of what reality is actually like. When we keep track like this, we're building up our belief in magick, which strengthens our ability to have even more magickal moments in our life.

Write about them in your journal, take photos, or as I did in this case, keep the fork, and share your experience with those who are open-minded and encouraging of your mystical endeavors.

Energy Ball Exercise

Sit comfortably in front of your altar with your working candle lit.

Breathe slowly and deeply, and as you do so, bring your awareness to the energy in your body.

Feel your energy moving through your feet, up your legs to your torso, and then to your chest, arms, neck, and head.

As you breathe, visualize a warm, glowing light at the center of your chest, around your heart area. Imagine this light growing brighter and expanding, filling your chest with energy.

Extend your hands in front of you, palms facing each other but not touching, keeping your fingers relaxed.

Imagine that the energy from your heart center is flowing down your arms and out through your palms, creating a ball of energy between your hands.

Slowly move your hands closer together and then apart, feeling the sensation of energy as if you were holding a ball. Notice what sensation comes up for you when you do this. What does this energy feel like? What temperature is it?

Experiment with the energy ball between your hands by moving it around. Make it larger by pulling your hands apart and then smaller again by bringing your palms closer together.

Once you feel comfortable doing this, hold the energy ball in the palm of one hand and make it expand and shrink back down to a smaller size by willing it to do so with your mind.

To finish the exercise, bring your hands together, allowing the energy ball to dissipate.

Close your eyes, take a few deep breaths, and make any notes from the experience in your magickal journal.

Expanding Your Personal Energy Field

Sit comfortably in front of your altar with your working candle lit.

As you did in the previous exercise, breathe slowly and deeply, and as you do so, bring your awareness to the energy in your body.

Feel your energy moving through your feet, up your legs to your torso, and then to your chest, arms, neck, and head.

As you breathe, visualize a warm, glowing light at the center of your chest, around your heart area. Imagine this light growing brighter and expanding, filling your chest with energy.

Then imagine this light expanding beyond your chest in front of you and behind your back, extending about 6 inches outside of your physical body.

With every inhale, imagine that you're gathering up energy from within your body and with every exhale, imagine that you're pushing the energy out through your heart center into the energy ball that's growing bigger around you.

Every time you exhale, imagine the energy growing until it's completely encompassing your body like a giant egg.

Continue expanding your energy until it fills the room you're sitting in, your entire home, neighborhood, city, country, and then beyond the entire planet.

Feel the oneness you have with all that is.

When you're ready to finish the exercise, imagine your energy shrinking back down with every exhale from encompassing the planet, to your country, city, neighborhood, home, room you're sitting in, and then bring the energy back into your body completely.

Energy Feeding

As energetic beings, we are in constant communication with all other energies in the Universe, and part of that communication can be 'feeding,' where we intentionally absorb the frequencies around us.

This can help us in our magickal practice as it builds up our auric field, trains us to be more intentional with energy flow, and helps us attune to specific frequencies.

We do this unintentionally all the time when we hug our pets or spend time with people who naturally light us up and leave us feeling energized after an encounter with them.

With this type of feeding, you are not stealing energy from people; you are being intentional with the direction of the energy that's radiating from others.

Going back to the pet example, when you hug your cat, you are not draining its life force; you are enjoying the benefits of the energy it's giving off.

I first noticed the potency of this exercise back in my 20s when I spent a lot of time in nightclubs. Even on the nights when I wasn't using substances, I'd find myself feeling a natural high after being in a large group of people.

I'd experience the same kind of energetic high during the drawn out, ecstatic worship services in the Pentecostal churches I attended off and on over the years when I was spiritually seeking.

This energy was most palpable in the strip clubs I went to regularly, where you could feel the lust emanating from both the women dancing and the members of the audience. It hung in the air ripe for the taking, and I always left those clubs feeling more alive than when I entered.

You can feed off of this psychic energy from a variety of sources:

• A crowd of people

- Individually from people you are physically close to

- Individually from people you are connecting with in the astral

- The elements

- The Universal field

Feeding off a Crowd

To feed off of a group of people, such as those gathered for a concert, sporting event, or at a nightclub, first set the intention that you will only absorb energies that are for your highest good and get yourself into the frequency that you want to take in.

If it's joy you want to experience more of, cultivate that feeling within by thinking of things that bring you joy. Do the same for love, peace, lust, or anything else you would like to amplify. If it's general life force energy you'd like to fill up on, set the intention that you will absorb that from the crowd.

Next, visualize this energy radiating from the crowd in the form of a mist, light, or smoke. See it rising up from the people and hanging in the air like a thick cloud.

Then imagine the pores of your skin opening up and absorbing some of this substance. Feel it moving all throughout your body until you are filled to capacity with the energy.

Alternatively, you can visualize the energy from the group entering through the top of your head at your crown chakra and then moving all throughout your body, filling you with the frequency that you desire to feel more of.

Your body will tell you when you have had enough, and at that point, visualize your pores or your crown chakra returning to normal.

Feeding off an Individual

To feed off another person you are with physically, you can do so by touching them with your receptive hand (this will be your left hand if you are right-handed) and imagining their energy moving into your body through that connection point.

See this energy as a glowing light, mist, or smoke circulating through the other person and coming into your body through your point of contact.

As you feed, you are opening up to them as well, sharing your energy. This merging creates more intimacy and a stronger bond between the two of you.

You can also perform this type of feeding in the astral if you can't be with the other person physically.

This can be great for couples in a romantic relationship who have to spend time apart yet still want to feel a close energetic tie to each other.

To astrally feed, get into a light meditative state and imagine the other person in the environment you think they'd be in at that time. Doing this exercise when you know the other person is asleep will be the easiest time to connect with them.

Visualize yourself astrally visiting this person as if you are there in the flesh. At first, look at this scene as if you are watching a movie where you are seeing the astral version of you walking into the room and approaching the person.

Once you've taken in the details of what the person looks like and you've had a look around the room, go from watching this scene like a movie to being in the movie as the astral version of yourself.

Touch the person with your receptive hand as you feel and see some of their life force energy moving through their body, transferring into your body through your hand. Visualize this energy coursing through your body and fully mixing with your own.

When you are finished, remove your hand, go back to watching the scene as if it's a movie, and see the astral version of you leave the room, coming back fully into your physical body.

Feeding off Elemental Energy

With this type of feeding, you will be increasing the frequency in your body associated with different natural elements and calling on the energy of Lucifer and the elemental demons.

If you want to feel more grounded and centered, you'll want to feed off of earth and call on Belial.

If you want to feel more connected to your emotions, feed off of water and call on Leviathon.

To strengthen your intuition or invite an influx of new ideas, feed off of air, and call on Lucifer.

And if you want to feel more passion or need an energetic push to fuel your actions, feed off of fire, and call on Flereous.

When you've chosen the element you want to absorb the properties of, go out into nature or bring some of that element into your home.

For earth, this can be simply walking outside to the nearest spot of bare ground, touching a tree, or working with a houseplant you already have inside.

To connect with water, you can head to a local stream, river, or pond, or venture to the nearest lake or ocean if you live close by.

To work with this element inside, you can gather rainwater or bring water from a natural source home in a jar. Bottled spring water or tap water can also work.

If your source is from a dug well, you can use it right away, but if you live in the city or have chemically treated water, leave it sitting out on your counter overnight to purify.

Air is the easiest element to connect with because all you have to do is be aware of its presence, whether you're indoors or outside.

To connect with fire, ensure that you're doing so in a safe way. If it's legal to have a small outdoor fire where you live, you can use that, or you can work with the flame of a candle.

To begin the feeding process, set the intention around the frequency that you'd like to embody on a deeper level with the help of the element.

Place your receptive hand on the element you're connecting with if possible.

For earth, you can place your hand on the ground, against a tree, or touch your fingers to the soil of your houseplant or dish of dirt gathered from outside.

If you're connecting with water, submerge your hand in it, or if you're using a smaller container, dip the tip of your finger in it.

To connect with air, whether you're outside or indoors, bring awareness to your receptive hand and notice the sensation you feel on your hand when you move it through the air or a breeze rushes over it.

With fire, you obviously won't be touching the element, but you can place your hand close enough to the flame where you can feel the warmth from it without jeopardizing your safety.

To feed off of the chosen element, imagine the properties of the earth, water, air, or fire rushing in through your receptive hand and filling up your entire body. As you do so, recite the enn of the demon associate with the element:

Earth/Belial: Lirach Tasa Vefa Wehlc Belial

Water/Leviathon: Jaden Tasa Hoet Naca Leviathan

Air/Lucifer: Renich Tasa Uberaca Biasa Icar Lucifer

Fire/Flereous: Ganic Tasa Fubin Flereous

Let your intuition guide you with the visual. You might see this energy flowing into you as the element itself; for example, with water, it could pool around your hand and then trickle into your body. Alternatively, it could flow into you as light or even with no visual representation at all.

Feeding off Universal Energy

Feeding from Universal energy regularly will help you feel energized, and it's a great way to help maintain an open channel for spirit communication as this energy also cleanses you as you feed.

You can perform this feeding at any time whether you're indoors or outside.

To begin, take a few deep breaths and if it's safe to do, close your eyes and meditate for a few moments to calm your mind and body.

Imagine a red light forming at the base of your tailbone where your root chakra is. As this light grows brighter, imagine two red cords coming out from the light, moving down each of your legs, through the bottom of your feet, down into the earth, and finally wrapping around the core of the earth.

With practice, you'll feel this grounding in your body. If you do this exercise with your feet on the floor, it will feel like they're suction-cupped to it. If you do the exercise sitting, you will feel a heaviness in your root chakra, as if it's stuck to the surface you're sitting on.

Next, imagine a golden light of Universal energy pouring in through the top of your head and moving down through your entire body. The source of this light is infinite, and you can drink in as much as you like.

As you feed, set the intention that the light will cleanse anything that needs to be removed from your energetic field.

To amplify this feeding practice, I visualize Lucifer standing beside me with his hand over my heart. The image I see when I do this is a burning flame in my chest that's being fueled with both Universal energy and Lucifer's divine light and power.

Chapter 9: Developing Your Psychic Senses

We're all born with natural psychic abilities, and developing them will enhance everything from your spirit communication and spellcasting to making aligned moves in all areas of your life.

Before we go any further, I want you to feel into the truth that you are already psychic. These abilities aren't reserved for a select few. Just like the other senses we have, psychic abilities come along with being human.

The problem is, most people shut down these abilities as they get older. Most of us attended schools where the emphasis was on absorbing information from 'experts', and we learned that if we wanted answers to something, it was best to seek those answers from an outside source.

Of course, there's a time and place for learning information from others, but you have an internal guidance system that gives you access to wisdom that's unique to you and your personal life path.

As a witch, growing in your psychic abilities will help you with:

Enhanced Perception: Developing your psychic abilities will enhance your perception beyond the ordinary senses. They'll help you access information or insights that are not readily available through the five senses, allowing for a deeper understanding of both the physical realm and spiritual realms.

Connection to the Demonic and Other Spirits: Whenever we're communicating with demons or other types of spirits, the connection we have with them is through our psychic abilities. The development of these senses will help you build stronger relationships with the demonic and make communication with them easier.

Divination and Insight: Whether you use divination tools such as the Tarot, bones, pendulums, or oracle cards, growing in your psychic abilities will help you gain insights into the future, understand hidden aspects of situations, and receive guidance from spiritual sources.

Energy Work: Developing your psychic abilities will give you a better understanding of how to work with and manipulate energy for healing, protection, and general magickal workings that you do.

Self-Discovery and Spiritual Growth: Psychic development is a path of self-discovery and spiritual growth. By honing these abilities, you'll gain a deeper understanding of yourself, your purpose, and your overall connection with the Universe.

Rituals and Spellwork: Psychic abilities can be seen as tools for more effective magickal rituals and spellwork. Sensing energy, visualizing outcomes, or tapping into intuitive insights can enhance the efficacy of magickal practices.

The four main psychic senses we'll be diving deeper into are:

1. Clairvoyance (Clear Seeing): The ability to receive information visually, often involving images or symbols. Clairvoyants may see visions or receive insights about people, places, or events.

2. Clairaudience (Clear Hearing): The ability to perceive sounds or auditory information beyond the normal range of hearing. Clairaudients may hear voices, sounds, or messages from spiritual sources.

3. Clairsentience (Clear Feeling): The ability to sense or feel information on an emotional or energetic level. Clairsentients may pick up on the emotions or energy associated with people, places, or events.

4. Claircognizance (Clear Knowing): The ability to receive information or knowledge without a clear logical reason. Claircognizants may have a strong sense of knowing something without having tangible evidence.

Most people notice that they're stronger in some of these ways of perceiving than others. My advice is to lean into the psychic sense that you're the strongest in while also training your other abilities.

Think of this like playing a musical instrument in a band. You can love music and have the ability to play any instrument, but if playing the piano comes the most easily and naturally to you, chances are you'll enjoy practicing it the most.

You can still develop your musical skills on other instruments, but when it comes time to perform, you know you're going to knock it out of the park on the piano because that's your go-to instrument.

This same idea applies to the divination tools and methods you use. You'll most likely be drawn to some more than others and enjoy practicing with those tools and methods.

In my own career as a witch, automatic writing, tarot, and oracle cards are the main methods I use to channel information. When I'm working with these, information pours through easily and activates my clairvoyance, which is my strongest clair, making it easy for me to relay messages to clients.

When practicing the exercises below to develop your psychic abilities, like with other metaphysical work you do, I encourage you to take it slow. Spending 20 minutes a day consistently will be much more effective than cramming in 4 hours of work once a week.

Similar to working out at the gym, achieving better results in psychic training involves consistent effort over several months, rather than attempting to do too much in a single session. Just as overtraining can lead to burnout in your physical body, pushing yourself too hard psychically can have similar consequences if you take on too much too soon.

With all of the exercises below, record your experiences in your magickal journal or in a separate journal devoted to your psychic development work.

Note down the date and time of day, the current moon phase and weather, and how you're feeling going into the exercise. Afterward, write down any messages that came through and how they came through (audible, visual, a general knowing, etc.) along with any other relevant details you want to keep track of.

If possible, do these exercises at your altar to build up psychic energy in your sacred space.

Strengthening Your Clairvoyance Abilities

Find a small, simple object in your home to work with, like an apple, a pen, or a spoon.

While sitting in a comfortable position, take a few deep breaths and look at the object. Pick it up and notice its appearance from all different angles.

Then close your eyes and look up toward your third eye. This is the spot on your forehead just above your eyebrows.

With your eyes still closed, mentally picture your chosen object. Visualize the object in as much detail as possible. Notice the color and texture as you mentally look at it from different angles with your mind's eye. Zoom in on certain areas of it and then zoom back out.

Practice holding the mental image of the object for as long as possible.

When you can easily visualize it, continue growing in this practice by repeating the exercise with different objects. As you advance, choose ones with more details.

You can also do this with people, your pets, a photo, and different areas in your home. Look at your chosen subject with your physical eyes, taking in as much detail as possible, then mentally recreate what you see in your mind's eye.

Strengthening Your Clairaudience Abilities

Find a comfortable position and take a few deep breaths.

Close your eyes and pay attention to the sounds you hear. These can be coming from inside your home, such as the sound from a furnace or appliances running, or outside from birds, traffic, or construction.

Keeping your eyes closed, focus on one specific sound you're hearing. Set the intention that you will only hear that one sound, and hear it getting progressively louder and louder until it drowns out everything else.

Repeat this process with other sounds you hear in your environment, setting the intention to dial up the volume on one sound at a time.

Once you've practiced with noises in your immediate environment, mentally picture a scene and imagine the noises that you'd hear if you were there in that physical place.

Start off with a tranquil place like a forest, beach, or meadow, imagining the sounds of birds, waves crashing, or the wind rushing through the long grass. Repeat the process of choosing one sound and turning up the volume on it. Then do the same

with the other sounds you think you'd be hearing in that location.

As you advance, go to imaginary environments with a greater variety of noises such as a coffee shop or an outdoor café in a busy city. After listening to the different sounds you hear in the location, focus on one at a time as in the previous versions of the exercise.

Strengthening Your Clairsentience Abilities

Gather together three different small objects to work with.

Choose one that still has strong life force energy, such as an apple, houseplant, or a freshly picked flower; one that's from nature, such as a rock, crystal, or piece of wood; and one that's been manufactured, like a plastic item or metal spoon.

Find a comfortable position and take a few deep breaths. Pick up one of the objects and hold it in your hands.

With your eyes closed, focus on how the energy of the object feels.

Pay attention to any intuitive feelings, gut reactions, or emotional responses that you may experience. Trust the information that comes to you, even if it seems subtle or unclear. Do this for each of the three items and write down the differences you notice in energy from them.

You can also practice developing your clairsentience by noticing how you feel around different people and how you feel when you're in different environments.

When I used to live in the city, I walked everywhere and noticed a distinct change in vibration when moving through different neighborhoods even though they were located within just a few blocks of each other.

If you've ever walked into a room after people have been fighting, you've probably noticed a dramatic change in the energy of the space. The expression 'you could cut the tension in the air with a knife' rings true because the energy in that environment is heavier than usual due to the frequency the people were emitting during the argument.

Strengthening Your Claircognizance Abilities

Find a comfortable position and take a few deep breaths.

Close your eyes and visualize a golden light opening at your third eye on your forehead right above your eyebrows. Mentally see this light shooting up and out into the cosmos creating a channel for information to easily flow to you.

Ask to receive the answer to a question you have and request that the answer be delivered through claircognizance. Stay open and relaxed without trying to force any messages to come through.

Pay attention to any impressions, insights, or thoughts that come to you. These may feel like sudden flashes of understanding or a strong sense of conviction. Write any messages in your journal and notice over the next few days if you receive any intuitive message related to your question.

I've found that with type of psychic sense, the answers often come through a short while after the exercise is performed such as when you're in the shower, doing dishes, or out for a walk on a familiar route.

When we're engaged in activities like this that we perform regularly, our conscious mind naturally goes on autopilot which opens us up to receive psychic information more easily.

To advance your practice, you can tune into your intuition and make predictions for which sports team is going to win the game before it starts, or predict the outcome of a tv show or movie before you begin watching it. Keep track of how many times your 'guesses' were correct and you'll be amazed at how accurate you are thanks to your claircognizance skills.

How Demons Can Help with Psychic Development

All of the information you want to receive psychically is already available to access in the Universal field.

Since demons rule over the different elemental forces within this Universal energy field, they can help strengthen your psychic abilities in the following ways:

As the ruler of Air, Lucifer can assist in the development of clairaudience by helping you open up to hear the information you want to access. Call on Lucifer to help put information into words that you can hear and easily understand.

As the ruler of Fire, Flereous can help you with clairvoyance by metaphorically burning through anything that's preventing you from clearly seeing what you want to psychically see.

As the ruler of Water, Leviathon can bring you closer in touch with your emotions, enhancing your clairsentience and ability to intuitively feel information.

As the ruler of Earth, call on Belial for assistance in developing your ability to have a grounded knowing of information through claircognizance.

For assistance from the demonic, simply request their help by saying something like:

'Lucifer, please open up my ability to hear any intuitive messages I'm meant to hear.'

'Flereous, please symbolically burn away anything that's preventing me from clearly seeing the information I'm meant to receive.'

'Leviathon, please help me feel the intuitive messages I'm meant to receive.'

'Belial, please strengthen my ability to know information in a deep, grounded way.'

Chapter 10: Casting a Demonic Circle

When we're casting a circle, we're creating a space between the realms that's inviting to the spirits. It acts as a portal to different realities and a space where we can intentionally balance our energy with the assistance of the demonic.

Ideally, you'll want a space that's approximately 9' in diameter as that gives you lots of room to move around in, but work with whatever area you have available.

If you have the ability to set up a permanent ritual space, you can use chalk or paint directly on the floor, or use stones to outline the perimeter.

Alternatively, you can use a piece of fabric or rope to create a circle and put it out of sight when you're using your space for other things.

Your altar, ideally positioned in the east, can sit inside the circle or just outside of it depending on the setup of your room. Refer to the section of this book on altar setup for more details on what to include on it.

To begin, stand facing the East and take a few deep breaths.

As you inhale, imagine the power of the earth rising up through your feet and visualize this energy as red light flowing into you. Feel the grounding energy of the earth flowing through your entire body as you take it in.

Set the intention that this grounding energy is cleansing you of anything that might stand in the way of your magick and connection with the demonic.

As you exhale, imagine any stale, stagnant energy leaving your body.

Once you feel grounded and centered (it will often feel like you've been suction-cupped to the floor by your feet), imagine a golden light coming from above and entering through the top of your head at your crown chakra.

As you inhale, imagine that you're being filled with the pure, cleansing energy of the cosmos and the divine light of Lucifer. Feel this light moving through the top of your head, all throughout your body, and mixing with the grounding energy of the earth.

As you exhale, imagine any stale, stagnant energy leaving your body.

Raise your hands from your sides up in a sweeping motion, and over your head as you say aloud,

'I stand between the realms, creator of my reality and weaver of my fate.'

Visualize yourself being surrounded by a powerful field of energy that radiates a few feet out from your body.

Still facing the East, say aloud,

'Lucifer of the East, I ask that you come and be present at this circle. Renich Tasa Uberaca Biasa Icar Lucifer!'

Feel the energy of air coming into the circle as a gust of wind. Imagine this wind filling your body with wisdom and knowledge.

Turn to face the South and say aloud,

'Flereous of the South, I ask that you come and be present at this circle. Ganic Tasa Fubin Flereous!'

Feel the energy of fire coming into the circle as warmth. Imagine this fire filling your body with passion and a lust for life.

Turn to the West and say aloud,

'Leviathon of the West, I ask that you come and be present at this circle. Jaden Tasa Hoet Naca Leviathon!'

Feel the energy of water coming into the circle as crashing sea waves. Imagine this water activating your emotions and opening you up to feel the fullness of life.

Turn to face the North and say aloud,

'Belial of the North, I ask that you come and be present at this circle. Lirach Tasa Vefa Wehlc Belial!'

Feel the energy of earth coming into the circle as rich soil. Imagine this earth energy creating a stable environment for your dreams and aspirations to take root.

Once all four demonic quarters have been called and you're feeling balanced, it's time to sit or stand at your altar, do any magickal work you feel called to do, or communicate with the spirits.

Standard Void Meditation to do Before Magick or Spirit Communication

Sit comfortably in front of your altar with your working candle lit and gaze softly at the flame for a few moments to bring your mind into focus.

Breathe slowly and deeply, inhaling for a count of 4, holding that breath for a count of 4, and exhaling for a count of 4.

Close your eyes and imagine yourself floating in complete darkness.

You are weightless and surrounded by the dark matter of creation. Imagine this infinite sea of darkness in front of you as far as you can, behind you, and on both sides of you.

You are one with this dark matter
One with the Void
One with the energy that creates all that is

Breathe deeply now at the pace your body wants to go, feeling your diaphragm expand as you inhale through your nose and contract as you exhale through your mouth.

Imagine with every inhale, you're breathing in energy from the Void. There is an infinite supply of this energy, and as it moves into your body, it's filling your cells with the creative force of the Universe itself.

As you exhale, imagine any stale, stagnant energy leaving your body through your mouth and immediately being transformed by the Void back into creative energy.

Perform this breathing exercise until it feels like you have cleared the stagnant energy from your body.

Chapter 11: Connecting with Lucifer and the Demonic

Contacting the demonic can occur without delving into meditation, learning how to work with energy, or creating sacred space. However, I've provided instructions on how to do all of these things first because a solid foundation in magickal basics will help you have a better and safer experience when working with entities.

To use the fitness example again, it's comparable to walking into a gym without ever having worked out before. While you can jump on the treadmill, run at full speed, and over-lift heavy weights, that's likely to leave you feeling incredibly sore the next day. Without taking the proper steps to build up your muscles and endurance, you may even end up injured.

Spiritual work follows a similar principle. Even if your physical body isn't in danger, you can burn out psychically and invite parasitic spirits into your space if you haven't built up a solid magickal practice through meditation and energy work.

If you've been progressing through the exercises in order, you've already prepared yourself for working more closely with the demonic specifically by meditating with their enns and casting a demonic circle.

The Connection Process

Cast your demonic circle, sit comfortably in front of your altar, and meditate for a few minutes to quiet your body and mind.

Enter your astral temple and see yourself in the room that you'd like to use for spirit communication.

Invite Lucifer into your temple space by stating aloud or in your mind,

'Lucifer, I call you forth. Come and be present in this temple.'

Then begin chanting his enn a few times: **'Renich Tasa Uberaca Biasa Icar Lucifer'**

Gaze at the image of Lucifer's sigil softly until the lines start to blur as you continue to repeat the enn Renich Tasa Uberaca Biasa Icar Lucifer.

Swaying back and forth gently will help you move deeper into a trance state, making the connection process easier.

Look to the door in your astral temple space that's devoted to the entry and exit of your spirit guests. Visualize Lucifer walking through the door and passing through a bright, white light.

Lucifer will appear to you in a form that's most useful for the relationship he has with you.

For some, he appears as a devilish creature, and for others, he looks more angelic, with every variation imaginable in between. There's no right or wrong way to visualize him; just let your imagination create the form it wants to.

Invite him to join you in your temple space and ask him any questions you might have. Share with him anything you want to that's on your mind, and feel what it's like to be in his presence.

Spirit communication will flow the easiest when you get out of your head and allow yourself to receive the messages that come through intuitively.

If you're naturally strong in clairaudience, you'll likely hear Lucifer speak to you.

If clairvoyance is your strength, you'll easily receive a mental picture of him and the things that he wants to show you.

If you're clairsentient, you will easily pick up on the frequencies that Lucifer wants to share with you, with the information coded in the feelings you get from him.

And if you're naturally claircognizant, you'll experience a deep knowing of what he's sharing without having the specifics of how the information came through.

The length of time you spend in direct communication with Lucifer will vary. It could just be a few seconds, or you might feel his presence for a longer period of time.

With practice, you'll be able to feel when the communication is over. It's important not to force the relationship or try to drag out the communication time.

The demonic are usually quite blunt and will tell you when they're finished with a meeting or when they don't want to be bothered connecting with you.

I've had multiple experiences of calling a demon and having them say, 'Seriously? We just talked about this yesterday. Quit wasting my time and call me when you've done what you said you were going to do.'

When it feels like the communication process has come to an end, imagine Lucifer walking back through the door he entered through inside of your astral temple, passing through a white light as he leaves.

Use this connection process for any other demon you'd like to form a working relationship with, substituting their name, demonic enn, and sigil.

If it doesn't feel like you've made a connection, take a break and come back to the exercise another day. You might just have to practice sensing spirits, or the particular demon you've called doesn't want to work with you at this point in time.

I've had this happen with Lilith in the past. I felt certain that it was time to work with her, but when I went through the connection process, I got a very clear 'no' from her, letting me know that it wasn't a good match for us to work together at that time.

As with other types of relationships, those that we want to have with the demonic shouldn't be forced (attempting to force a demon into working with you is a great way to have a terrifying experience with them).

To ensure I'm getting a 'yes' from the demon I feel called to work with, once I invite them into my astral temple, I'll ask them if they want to form a working relationship. If I don't sense a clear yes or no, I'll use a pendulum to get an accurate answer and either continue with the communication process or thank them for their presence and have them leave.

Demonic Offerings

Making regular offerings to the demonic can enhance your relationship with the specific demons you're working with, show your appreciation to the demonic forces, and strengthen your connection to their realm in general.

In my practice, I offer water, fresh flowers, tea, incense, gratitude, public acknowledgement, sexual fluids, or blood.

I place these items on my altar or on the demon's sigil along with a simple prayer to the demonic like **'Thank you for your guidance, wisdom, and protection'**, and if it's a specific goal they've helped me with, I'll mention that in the prayer.

For public recognition, I'll mention the demon in social media posts and sometimes share the details of how they've helped me. This form of offering works well because public acknowledgment feeds more energy to the demon, can help others gain a better understanding of who the demonic are, and draws those who are meant to work with them.

If you're using water, food, or flowers, replace the offering regularly to keep it fresh and if you do want to offer blood or sexual fluids, do your research to ensure the demon you're working with appreciates that kind of thing.

Channeling Spirit Messages Through Automatic Writing

Automatic writing is an effective way to channel messages from the spirits you work with, and like other forms of psychic development, the more you practice, the easier it gets.

With automatic writing, you're physically moving the pen on paper, or typing on a keyboard, but the words flowing through you aren't your own; they're coming from the spirit you've intended to receive messages from.

To begin, know which spirit you want to channel messages from. Ideally, choose a demon that you already feel a connection with.

Cast a demonic circle and sit comfortably in front of your altar with a pen and notebook with you.

You probably won't want to use your magickal journal for this because you'll be filling pages with scribbles and a lot of messy writing.

To begin the automatic writing process, take a few deep breaths and connect with the demon you want to communicate with.

When you feel their presence, close your eyes and start drawing circles and loops in your notebook to get the flow of writing started. By drawing these loops and scribbles, you'll relax your conscious mind and enable the spirit to speak through you more easily.

Ask the spirit any questions you have as you continue to draw loops and scribbles on the paper. A moment will come when the communication clicks in, and you'll start to write actual words.

When I do this, the words are usually illegible because my pen can't keep up with the flow of the messages. If you find this is happening for you, recite the messages into a voice note app on your phone as they come through, rewrite them immediately after your channeling experience, or switch to typing the messages.

When using a laptop to take down the messages, begin the exercise by typing random letters on the keyboard to get your hands relaxed and fingers used to dancing over the keys. Then proceed to ask the spirit questions and let their energy transmit the messages through you.

Using a Scrying Mirror for Spirit Communication

Scrying mirrors can be used for divination as well as spirit communication. This tool will be especially effective if you're naturally clairvoyant and receive psychic messages through visual images easily.

You can purchase scrying mirrors from occult shops and artists, or you can make your own using a few items from the dollar store.

To make your own scrying mirror, you'll need:

- A picture frame with a glass plate (the standard 8x10 size works well)
- Black spray paint or acrylic craft paint and a brush
- Newspapers or something to protect your work surface

Remove the glass plate from the picture frame and wipe it clean.Place it down on the newspapers and paint one side of it black. Apply enough coats of paint to ensure a smooth, opaque finish.

When the paint is dry, place the glass back inside the picture frame with the unpainted surface facing out.

To work with your mirror, place it on your altar to charge with demonic energy for at least a day. When you're ready to use it for communication, place it in front of where you're seated with a candle on each side.

Connect with the demon you'd like to communicate with, relax your eyes, and gaze softly into the mirror.

Be open to any images you see coming through. You might see a physical representation of the spirit you're working with or other visuals the demon is using to communicate. Make any notes from your experience in your magickal journal.

Chapter 12: Manifesting Your Will

You can be, do, and have anything that you desire in this life, and magick can help you make those dreams a reality.

It will still require work on your part in the mundane world, of course, but magick can make things happen easier and faster, and the spirit realm can be called upon for various forms of support.

When you tap into the Luciferian current by forming a relationship with Lucifer and the demonic, you'll find that while the journey won't always be comfortable, you'll be able to manifest more than you ever dreamed possible.

Lucifer liberates us from the self-imposed limitations that keep us in bondage, illuminates the things that we hold in the shadows, and guides us on our path as we bring our desires to life.

In order to get the best results from any spellwork you do with Lucifer and the demonic, you need to have a clear vision for what you're manifesting, align your internal state with your desires, and show up in the world as the version of you who's already manifested the result you want to achieve from your spellwork.

Before heading to the altar to perform spells, I recommend starting with the creation of a big picture vision that you want to have for your life. This should take into account the work you do in your business or career, your relationships, where you live, physical fitness goals, and your spiritual development.

From this bigger picture vision, it will be easier to determine the magick that will best support the manifestation of the smaller goals that go into the creation of your chosen reality.

Crafting Your Life Vision

For this exercise, take a piece of paper and mark out three columns. At the top of the first column, write BE; at the top of the second column, write DO; and for the third, write HAVE.

List out absolutely everything you can think of under each category that you'd like to manifest in your life.

What do you want to BE? A good singer, more confident, or the CEO of your company?

What do you want to DO? Travel to Europe, learn how to speak a new language, or go sky diving?

What do you want to HAVE? A new car, your own animal rescue, or a greenhouse to grow food in year round?

Take as much time as you need with this. After all, this is your life you're designing.

Once you've gotten everything down on paper, visualize yourself living this life.

See and feel yourself in this experience in as much detail as possible. Allow yourself to become fully immersed in this vision just like you would in a movie.

Here are some questions to help guide you in this process:

Where are you living in this ideal reality?
What does your home look like and how is it decorated?
Do you live in the city or country?
If you see yourself driving a car, what kind is it?
Who are you with and what are your interactions with these people like?
What are you doing for work?
What does your body look like and feel like?
What foods are you eating, and what do you do for exercise?
How are you spending your leisure time?
What books are you reading?
What podcasts are you listening to?
What movies and TV shows do you watch?
What kind of conversations are you having with people?
How do you feel during your day?
What does your spiritual practice look like?

Are you traveling? If so, what kind of hotels do you stay in and what parts of the world do you visit?

How is your relationship with your friends, family, and what do you enjoy doing together?

To expand upon this vision and reveal things that you might be limiting yourself from, call on Lucifer to guide you with this process and say aloud:

'Lucifer, show me what's possible. Illuminate this grand vision I have for my life and reveal to me anything that's missing.'

Be open to any messages that come through from him and add any new elements into your bigger picture vision as you see fit.

Now that you have a general idea of what your dream life looks like, it's time to narrow things down into what you can see yourself manifesting within the next year.

This will help you ground this new reality into your current day-to-day life and ensure this doesn't just stay a fantasy that you'd like to experience 'someday', which we know is a day that never comes.

Then break down the things you want to manifest into categories: business or career, relationships, spiritual development, health and fitness, etc.

Also, look for elements of your bigger picture vision that you can incorporate right now.

For instance, if you see yourself living in a mansion on the beach but right now you're living in a studio apartment with no idea how you'd afford such a home, that goal will probably feel distant and unattainable.

You can, however, bring some elements into your current reality to move deeper into the bigger picture vision. For example, if you imagine having fresh flowers on the kitchen table of your beach house, you can buy yourself a bouquet of flowers to put on the kitchen table in your current apartment.

Start with where you are and add in smaller pieces from your dream life.

If you envision yourself having a personal trainer that you work out with three times a week but that's not in your budget right now, find a free workout plan online and start doing home workouts.

If you envision yourself eating only organic foods, start with buying one or two organic items when you hit the grocery store. For each goal, mentally see the version of you who's already in that experience and create a mini-mind movie with you being the main character living in that reality.

Whatever the goal is, create a mental image you feel emotionally connected to that will be happening once the goal has manifested.

For example, when I'm manifesting a new money goal, I don't get lit up just by seeing a number in my bank account. While I might visualize that once in a while to normalize having the new number in my account, I'll also focus on what that money will help me be, do, and have.

Since I love New Orleans, I'll often imagine myself walking through the streets of the French Quarter because the money I'm manifesting can go toward a trip there.

I'll create a couple of different mini-mind movies to really get into what that experience is like.

In one, I see myself sitting at Cafe Du Monde early in the morning while it's still dark out, sipping on their delicious coffee and eating a beignet while I journal.

In another, I'm watching the sunrise over the Mississippi, this time with my coffee in a takeout cup, and hearing the water splash up against the riverbed while the crow that's been following me since I left my hotel caws in the background.

Along with seeing myself in these scenes, I incorporate my other senses to completely immerse myself into the vision.

This is key because our brain doesn't know the difference between what's real and what's imaginary, and the more 'real' your manifestation feels for you, the easier it's going to become your reality.

Using the New Orleans example, I'll imagine the smell of the coffee, the heat of it hitting my lips, and the sweetness of the powdered sugar from the beignets. I'll feel the mugginess in the air and the cobblestone streets under my feet as I walk.

Once you have a clear mental image for each of your goals, write out the details of each one in your magickal journal.

To make this exercise even more powerful, create a vision board with pictures that represent the different things you're manifesting.

If a trip to Paris is something on your list of dream destinations, find a picture with the Eiffel tower in it. If it's a new car, find an image of the exact model, in your preferred color.

You can create a vision board digitally using a free design website like Canva and gathering images you find online, or you can go the old school route by cutting out pictures from magazines or printing pictures from your computer and gluing them to a piece of cardboard.

Building a Magickal Mindset

Your mindset is comprised of the thoughts you think and the beliefs you hold to be true about yourself and the world around you (beliefs are thoughts you've practiced thinking over and over again).

You think thousands of thoughts per day, with the majority being the same ones day after day, and they run like background music in your mind. You're so used to playing these thoughts on repeat that unless you make a conscious effort to notice them and shift them, they'll continue running like bad elevator music.

The worst part about these thoughts is that a lot of them aren't even yours.

When we're young, up until the age of 5-7, we don't have the ability to mentally filter what we're picking up from the world around us.

Without a mental filter to determine what you want to believe, you'd hear someone say something, and it would automatically register in your mind as the truth.

These thoughts and beliefs could be from your parents and caregivers, TV and movies, religious programming if you went to church, and from other outside sources you were exposed to.

This means if you heard your parents arguing or stressing out over money, for example, you're probably holding onto stories about money that aren't even true, such as:

Money doesn't grow on trees
Rich people are greedy assholes
Money is the root of all evil
Good people work hard for their money

The same thing applies for every other area of life. If you grew up hearing things like:

It's hard to find a good man
All women are gold diggers
It's hard to lose weight
Once you hit 40 you're over the hill

Chances are those beliefs stayed with you into adulthood unless you had contrary evidence through your own lived experiences.

In order to see exactly how your thoughts are creating your reality, pick something from your big picture vision in step one that you're manifesting.

We'll use money as an example because a lot of people want more of that.

Grab a pen and paper and finish each of the following prompts as many times as you can:

Money is…
Making money is…
Receiving money easily is…
People with a lot of money are…
People who don't have a lot of money are…

Even if you don't want to believe the things you wrote down, those are the thoughts that are shaping your self-concept and your ability to manifest more money.

Do this type of journaling exercise for the other areas of life you've set goals in as well to uncover what you believe to be true about having what you want in your relationships, your health and fitness, your family, spiritual life, career, or business.

Next, open your mind up to new possibilities by getting curious and for each belief you wrote down, ask:

Is this ultimately true?
Is it possible that there are people in this world who think differently about this?
If I were to choose to believe something different, what would that be?

Call on Lucifer for guidance by saying **'Lucifer, help me see things differently. What else could I believe about this that would support the manifestation of my desires?'**

Quantum Magick

Before getting into specific rituals you can do to manifest your goals, I'll share a process that you can use at any time to connect

with the quantum field to bring your dreams to life. This can be incorporated with other rituals or used on its own to produce results.

Our entire Universe is one big energetic web where everything is connected to everything else, all at once. The past, present, and future are all happening right now and every possible scenario that you can dream of is also happening right now in another dimension.

Thankfully, we have time and space to keep us from experiencing all of this at once. If we were to experience everything without time and space being a factor, we wouldn't be able to handle it. That would be like going to a restaurant, ordering one of everything on the menu and trying to eat it all, all at the exact same time.

What we can do, however, is focus on the possibilities that we'd like to be true for us. These are the goals you created when you got clear on your overall life vision.

This process involves meditation and visualization.

If you're brand new to meditation, practice the different exercises given in the earlier chapter on the topic and work your way up to meditating in the Void.

It's ideal that you do this Quantum Magick meditation early in your day. If possible, do this exercise before you check your email and social media, before your kids or partner get up, and before you have a chance to settle into who you think you are.

Have a journal close by to record anything from the experience you want to make note of, or set up an audio recorder on your phone or computer so you can verbally make notes.

Sit comfortably in front of your altar with your working candle lit and gaze softly at the flame for a few moments to bring your mind into focus.

Breathe slowly and deeply, inhaling for a count of 4, holding that breath for a count of 4, and exhaling for a count of 4.

Close your eyes and imagine yourself floating in complete darkness.

You are weightless and surrounded by the dark matter of creation. Imagine this infinite sea of darkness in front of you as far as you can, behind you, and on both sides of you.

You are one with this dark matter
One with the Void
One with the energy that creates all that is

Breathe deeply now at the pace your body wants to go, feeling your diaphragm expand as you inhale through your nose and contract as you exhale through your mouth.

Imagine with every inhale, you're breathing in energy from the Void. There is an infinite supply of this energy and as it moves into your body, it's filling your cells with the creative force of the Universe itself.

As you exhale, imagine any stale, stagnant energy leaving your body through your mouth and immediately being transformed by the Void back into creative energy.

Perform this breathing exercise until it feels like you have cleared the stagnant energy from your body.

Sit in the Void breathing comfortably and then start to feel your energy moving through your body from your feet up to the top of your head. You might see this energy as a specific colour or feel a change in your body temperature.

Then imagine this energy extending out of your body through your third eye, the spot located on the center of your forehead just above your eyebrows. Visualize this energy forming an oval portal out in front of you, extending a few feet beyond your physical body.

Inside this portal of energy, imagine one of your mini-mind movies playing that show you already having manifested your goal. Watch yourself living in this new reality, in as much detail as possible.

Notice how you're moving, who you're with, what your environment is like, and feel what it's like to be this experience.

Then imagine yourself stepping into the portal with this other version of yourself. Walk over to this 'you' that you've been watching until you're close enough to fully merge with them. You are now one with the version of you who already has what you desire, who has already manifested the goal.

Take a moment to feel the energy in your body. Does it feel different after merging with this next-level version of you?

Are you receiving any psychic images? Are you hearing anything? Is there something you simply know now that you've merged with this version of you?

Write down anything that's coming through intuitively or speak it aloud if you're using a voice recorder.

Take a few moments to live in this mini-mind movie and feel what the experience is like. Place your awareness on your heart center and feel the experience as deeply as possible, as if it were happening right now in the present moment.

What you're doing here is using both your mental ability to send a clear picture to the energetic field of what you desire, and you're magnetizing it to you with the energy of your heart.

When you do this, you are moving yourself onto the frequency of where this reality already exists.

When you feel ready to end this exercise, say aloud, or in your mind:

'This is now my reality. This is who I am. It is done, it is done, it is done.'

A good time to end this visualization is when you no longer feel connected to it and it feels difficult to hold the mental picture in your mind.

Remember that this is a practice and you might only be able to visualize something for 10-15 seconds.

Know that whatever length of time you can hold it for is enough, and that with repetition, you'll be able to focus on mental pictures in your mind for longer periods of time, and with more intensity.

A portion of the population can't mentally 'see' images. If that's you, this will still work. Instead of visualizing yourself in the scenario, speak your intentions aloud, and focus on the feeling of the experience with your heart.

The key to the successful manifestation of your will is knowing that you are the source of everything you desire and that in order to experience what you want, you get to become it first internally.

This is what you've done in the above exercise. You cultivated the feelings of the experience you want to manifest before actually being there in the physical realm.

Strategy

Once you've gotten clear on what you want to manifest, and you've aligned your energy with your desires by feeling what that experience is like, you'll want to take action in the physical realm. This is where the strategy or the 'how' of manifestation comes into play.

For this part of the process, you're going to go to your astral temple and meet with the version of you that's already manifested the result you want to create.

Once you're in your astral temple, think of a specific goal you're working on and ask to meet with the 'you' who's already achieved it. Imagine this version you walking into your temple space though the same door you have spirits enter through, and invite them into conversation.

Interview this future version of you and ask them any questions you'd like about how they achieved the goal.

Here are some questions to ask them:

What were the biggest steps you took to create this result?
What was the very first step you took to manifest this goal?
How did you get over the fear of starting?
Who did you lean on for support?
How did you create the motivation to keep going?

You can also talk with this future version of you to get more clarity on the thoughts and feelings they practiced to help them manifest the goal.

Depending on your preferred method of receiving psychic messages, you may hear spoken words, see the information they want to convey to you, or simply have a general knowing encoded with the relevant information.

Record everything this next-level (or future) version of you shares, and then execute on the actions they give you.

You can come back and do this as often as you need to.

One thing to keep in mind is the importance of taking actions that move you deeper into your bigger picture vision even if they don't make sense from where you are right now.

Your destiny will pull you out of your comfort zone, and magick happens when you take actions knowing that you will be successful no matter what.

Incorporating Demons into Your Manifestation Practice

Once you've practiced the inner workings of magick outlined above, it's time to incorporate help from the demonic realm.

Demons can help us see things from different perspectives because they're not bound to human form like we are, and with their unique perspective, they can offer us guidance and support as we bring our desires to life.

For this practice, have a particular goal in mind that you'd like to manifest. Also have your journal or something to take notes with nearby to record any messages you receive from the demons.

Cast a demonic circle and sit comfortably in front of your altar.

Go into your astral temple and call upon the demons of the four elements to join you inside your temple.

I like to say something like **'Lucifer, I request your guidance and support. Please come into this temple'**. Followed by his demonic enn, **'Renich Tasa Uberaca Biasa Icar Lucifer.'** Chant the enn a few times until you feel the spirit connection has been made.

Then visualize Lucifer coming into your astral temple and joining you. If you have a specific room in your temple that you meet with spirit guides, visualize him moving to that space.

Repeat the process for the other demons.

'Flereous, I request your guidance and support. Please come into this temple. Ganic Tasa Fubin Flereous'

'Leviathon, I request your guidance and support. Please come into this temple. Jaden Tasa Hoet Naca Leviathan'

'Belial, I request your guidance and support. Please come into this temple. Lirach Tasa Vefa Wehlc Belial'

When your demonic council has been gathered, tell them about the goal you're manifesting in as much detail as possible. Let them know if you're struggling with anything in regards to it, and the progress you've made so far.

Say aloud **'Spirits that are gathered here today, help me see what I must see, and help me be what I must be to manifest my deepest desires.'**

Consult your demonic council and ask for any guidance or support they can offer based on their area of expertise.

Lucifer is associated with the element of air and can help you access new ideas and plans, clear your mind of confusion, align your thoughts with your desires, and he can help shed light on your path by showing you aspects of yourself or the situation that need illumination.

Flereous is associated with fire and can help you metaphorically burn through your self-imposed limitations or bridges from your past, and he can help you build up the inner fire required to fuel the actions you're taking.

Leviathon is associated with water and can help you access hidden emotional blocks you might have surrounding the manifestation of your goals, and he can guide you deeper into your feelings so you can more easily access the frequency of your desires.

Belial is associated with earth and can help you sort out the practical actions needed to bring your dreams to fruition, and assist you with grounding in new habits and behaviours.

Talk with your demonic council the same way you would with a trusted team of advisors. They're here to support you and can offer valuable insights.

As with any type of spirit communication, don't just do something because a spirit told you to do it. Run any advice or insight through your own lens of values and ensure any action you're taking feels truly aligned for you.

Record any notes that come through during your council meeting, thank the demons for their support, and have them leave your astral temple through the door designated for spirit guests.

The Demonic and Dark Alchemy

One of the most beautiful and also most difficult parts of the Luciferian path is the dark alchemy that we go through when we commit to our spiritual growth and evolution.

A lot of people come to the path of witchcraft and Luciferianism to gain. They want to manifest more money, love, sex, and enjoy the material pleasures that go along with living deliciously. All of these are wonderful and enhance our human experience.

However, most people seek these things as a source for validation and as a way to prove to themselves and others that they're successful. They look at the external markings of success to provide them with something it never will - true fulfillment and a deeper connection to their own personal power.

Chasing success only leads to more chasing because once you hit a goal or acquire that which you think will be the thing that makes you feel better, the satisfaction only lasts a moment. Then you're back to chasing more to get your fix. It's just like how an addict is constantly chasing the next high, hoping it will satisfy, only to be left wanting more.

The solution to having what you want and living a life that's filled with pleasure is going within and realizing that you are the source of all that you seek.

And this is the work that is wildly uncomfortable.

Because once we realize that the outer world isn't our source of safety, freedom, love, abundance, and validation, we're confronted with the very real fact that we have been giving our power away and playing the role of victim to our circumstances. If you choose to walk through the fire of transformation to find your true power, you need to face the parts of yourself that have given that power over to others.

You will come face to face with your shadow and own darkness, confronted with the beliefs and paradigm you've been operating in, and given the choice to either evolve and change or live out more of the same experiences.

Lucifer and the demonic can help you through this process by showing you what you need to see and change within yourself in order to have the life you want, but be prepared to get uncomfortable.

You will be required to raise your standards, stop engaging in certain behaviors, do things that are outside of your comfort zone, set boundaries, and say no to things your mind and body want to say yes to.

To do this shadow work with Lucifer and the demonic, think about an area you want to grow in, using your list of goals you've created from your life vision as a guide.

In your astral temple, meet with your demonic council and ask them to show what you've been hiding from yourself in regards to manifesting that goal.

After you've made your request, be open to messages from your council coming through in different ways. They might show you a memory from the past, a habit or behavior you need to change, or a relationship you're in that's hindering your growth.

The messages you're given might be obvious, or you might be shown more subtle things that are revealed with more depth over time.

After doing this work with the demonic, pay close attention to how you seek escape and comfort in your day-to-day life.

When you get lost in mindset scrolling on social media, what are you avoiding?

When you reach for another drink or more food when you're already full, what feeling are you numbing?

Where are you seeking validation from others?

Where are you not following through on promises you've made to yourself?

In what areas are you manipulating or trying to control others for your own benefit?

The answers to these questions will reveal the areas that you need to work on.

If you're struggling with making changes, call on the demonic for guidance and support. Personally, I've always found them to be brutally honest and not the type of entities to turn to if you're looking for a shoulder to cry on, but they will guide you on the path, and through the fire of transformation that will lead you deeper into your own power.

Chapter 13: Ritual and Spellwork

When we're performing rituals and casting spells, we're working with the natural forces that exist in our Universe to bend and shape our reality to produce a specific outcome.

While we can do that using the manifestation process outlined in the previous chapter, ritual and spellwork connect us more deeply with the spirit realm and can move us into the required inner state for magick more easily.

Whenever you're using ritual and spellwork to manifest a goal, incorporate the inner work outlined in the previous manifestation process for the best results.

To enhance your magick and work with the energies of the planets, time your spells so they're performed during the moon phase and day of the week that best fits your desired outcome.

The best days of the week for different types of workings:

Sunday (Sun):
Ideal for spells related to success, personal power, confidence, and healing. Works well for spells to boost your vitality, motivation, and leadership qualities.

Monday (Moon):
Perfect for spells involving emotions, intuition, psychic abilities, and dreams. Use for spells related to family, fertility, feminine energy, and purification.

Tuesday (Mars):
Suitable for spells involving courage, strength, protection, and physical energy. Use for spells related to ambition, conflict resolution, and assertiveness.

Wednesday (Mercury):
Ideal for spells involving communication, intellect, travel, and divination. Works well for spells related to education, problem-solving, and negotiation.

Thursday (Jupiter):
Perfect for spells related to abundance, wealth, expansion, and growth. Use for spells to enhance opportunities, luck, and spiritual growth.

Friday (Venus):
Suitable for spells involving love, romance, beauty, and relationships. Ideal for spells related to self-love, harmony, and enhancing your attractiveness.

Saturday (Saturn):
Ideal for spells involving protection, banishing, discipline, and transformation. Use for spells related to career advancement, long-term goals, and breaking bad habits.

To work with the moon's energy, here are the different phases and best types of magickal working for each:

New Moon:
Ideal for new beginnings, setting intentions, and starting projects. Use for spells related to personal growth, manifestation, and initiating change.

Waxing Crescent (1-49% illuminated):
Good for spells that involve growth, expansion, and attracting things into your life. Use for spells related to increasing abundance, love, or opportunities.

First Quarter (50% illuminated):
Suitable for spells that require action, determination, and overcoming obstacles. Use for spells related to achieving goals, breaking bad habits, and making decisions.

Waxing Gibbous (51-99% illuminated):
Good for spells focused on refinement, progress, and fine-tuning existing plans. Use for spells related to career advancement, creativity, and personal development.

Full Moon:
The most potent time for all types of spells, as the moon's energy is at its peak. Suitable for spells of all kinds, but especially for those that require maximum power, clarity, and completion.

Waning Gibbous (51-99% illuminated):
Ideal for spells that involve releasing, letting go, and shedding negative influences. Use for spells related to breaking curses, banishing, and cleansing.

Last Quarter (50% illuminated):
Good for spells that involve introspection, assessment, and eliminating obstacles. Use for spells related to inner reflection, resolving conflicts, and making amends.

Waning Crescent (1-49% illuminated):
Suitable for spells that focus on closure, rest, and tying up loose ends. Use for spells related to forgiveness, endings, and releasing past attachments.
(ChatGPT, 2023)

Demonic Sigil Spell

One of the simplest spells you can perform is to request assistance from the demonic realm and channel your intention into a demon's sigil.

There is a multitude of demons available for different purposes, but I recommend building a strong relationship with a small handful of them rather than adopting the 'dial a demon' approach. Of course, this is completely up to you, but I view our connection with the spirit realm similar to our relationships with other humans.

If I were to call up a stranger whom I heard was skilled at something I needed help with, there's a chance they might lend a hand, but my odds would be much better if I reached out to someone I already knew and had an established connection with.

Start working with Lucifer, Flereous, Leviathan, and Belial if they're cooperative with you, and then branch out from there.

If there's another demon you're meant to work with, they will make their presence known and come to you in dreams, meditation, or in your waking life, giving you a clear sign that they want to form a relationship with you.

For this type of spell, get clear on what you want to manifest and choose the demon you are intuitively drawn to work with, keeping in mind the areas that Lucifer, Flereous, Leviathon, and Belial are known for helping people with as discussed in previous chapters.

Draw their sigil on a piece of paper and, as you gaze at it, imagine being in the end result of your spell.

If it's more money you desire, create a clear mental picture of what having that money will look like, how you'll be spending it, and how you'll feel knowing that it's already in your bank account.

If you're manifesting more dates, picture yourself going out to your favorite restaurant, going for walks, or enjoying some bedroom activities with your new partner(s).

Immerse yourself in the vision of what will be happening when the spell is complete.

As you feel the energy of this desire being fulfilled in your body, let it build up and then channel this energy through your arms, out through your hands, and into the sigil.

Continue gazing softly at the sigil, seeing the lines blur together, deepening the trance state you're in.

When you do this, you're merging with demonic energy, sending out your intention to a specific demon. As you develop relationships with the demonic, it will be easier to receive communication from them, so have your journal handy or something to write down any insights that come through during the working.

When you're finished, there are a few options to choose from:

- You can anoint the sigil with a drop of your blood or bodily fluid and keep it on your altar until your goal has manifested. This is different than making an offering to a demon. You are adding your life force energy through the use of your fluids as an act of commitment to your goal.

- You can burn the sigil and use the ashes to anoint a candle or add them to a magickal oil.

- You can simply dispose of the sigil in the trash.

When working with demonic sigils, they act as portals of communication. You are not harming a demon by burning their sigil or being disrespectful to the demon by throwing out the paper their sigil is drawn on.

Candle Spells

Basic candle spells can produce exceptional results and are the entry point into magick for many witches.

There is a variety of candle sizes and styles to choose from that you can purchase from your local occult shop, online, or even from the dollar store.

Small chime candles are easy to work with as they're large enough to carve sigils into or write inscriptions on, yet small enough to burn down within an hour or two.

Figure candles are great if you want to incorporate more symbolism into your work. You can get them in a variety of colors and shapes that represent the work you're doing.

You can use a male or female figure candle to represent yourself or someone else, a couple facing each other to bring in a relationship, or a couple facing apart to help with a separation. There are also penis and vulva candles for sexual work, cat-shaped candles for good luck, and skulls for work focusing on the mind.

If you prefer longer workings, you can purchase 7-day candles that come in a glass holder. Some types are removable, which is great if you want to inscribe your candle, or you can draw sigils with a marker on the glass candle holder.

Below is a list of candle colors associated with different types of workings. Choose the best one for the spell you want to perform, and if you're unable to get one in the appropriate color, use a plain white candle.

White: Purity, cleansing, protection, healing, spirituality.

Black: Absorbing and banishing negativity, protection, warding off evil, and hexing.

Red: Love, passion, strength, courage, energy, vitality.

Pink: Romantic love, friendship, compassion, emotional healing.

Blue: Communication, wisdom, truth, protection, calmness.

Green: Abundance, prosperity, fertility, growth, money matters.

Yellow: Intellect, creativity, confidence, success, communication.

Purple: Psychic abilities, spiritual awareness, wisdom, intuition.

Orange: Creativity, attraction, success, energy, ambition.

Brown: Grounding, stability, home, finding lost items.

Gold: Wealth, prosperity, success, enlightenment, masculine energy.

Silver: Lunar magick, intuition, dreams, feminine energy, psychic abilities.

For a simple candle spell, place the candle on your altar in a fire-safe holder, light the wick, and as you gaze softly into the flame, visualize your desired outcome in as much detail as possible.

Let the dance of the flame move you deeper into a trance state where you feel as if you're shifting between the realms of your current reality and the one where your goal has manifested.
See yourself living in the end result of the spell and cultivate the feeling within yourself that you'll be experiencing.

Perhaps it's relief, joy, gratitude, love, or confidence. As the candle burns down, flood your body with this emotion, bringing in as many of your senses as possible to deepen the experience and make it feel real.

Depending on the size of your candle and the amount of time you can hold focus, you might have to break up your spell over a few days. It's better to have your candle spell run its course over a few days where you're able to hold your focus for 5-10 minutes at a time than spend an hour sitting in front of it with a wandering mind.

Here are some things you can do to expand beyond the basic candle spell:

Inscribe your candle with the sigil of the demon you'd like to call on for support with your working, or place a piece of paper with the demon's sigil underneath the candle (for safety, put a plate between the candle holder and paper).

Anoint the candle with your blood, saliva, sexual fluids, or a magickal oil.

If you work with herbs or powders, dress the candle with a small amount of oil and press the ground herbs or powder into the candle.

Write out a statement of intent for your spell, create a sigil based on that, and carve the sigil into the candle (sigil construction is covered in the Sex Magick chapter).

When your candle has burned down, the spell is complete and you can dispose of the wax in the trash.

Chapter 14: Sex Magick

Sexual energy is the potent force of creation itself and can be used to fuel your magickal workings. This energy is readily accessible, powerful enough to create human life, and becomes an effective tool when directed toward your goals, yielding astounding results.

Working with Lucifer may make it easier for you to connect with your sexual energy, as Lucifer is associated with the planet Venus—the planet governing love, pleasure, and sensuality.

Sex magick can be performed alone, with a partner, or in a group setting. If you are new to the practice, it is advisable to start solo until you grasp how to work with and control this energy for magickal purposes before exploring partnerships or group rituals. When working with other people or using their sexual fluids in your rituals, always ensure you're being safe to prevent the spread of disease.

The potency of sex magick lies in the fact that, during orgasm, you become a wide-open channel of power. At that moment, any blocks, fears, or limitations hindering the manifestation of a specific outcome are absent, allowing you to send a crystal-clear signal to the Universe about your desires.

Actively stirring up sexual energy without releasing it is also a powerful method to fortify your energetic field. Strengthening your aura makes it easier to shield yourself from negative energy, both in the physical and spirit realms. Since we manifest with our personal energy field, a more robust aura enables you to channel more power into your spellwork.

Conjuring and Harnessing Your Sexual Energy

For this exercise, you'll be arousing yourself without reaching orgasm.

If possible, conduct this work in your sacred space by casting a demonic circle, and sit or lie down comfortably in front of your altar. If privacy issues prevent this, find a location where you won't be interrupted.

Commence self-stimulation and pay attention to how your sexual energy feels as it moves through your body. Breathe slowly and deeply, visualizing this energy moving from your genitals through your body, reaching the top of your head, and then cycling back down.

Envision this energy flowing like an electric circuit, looping from your genitals to the top of your head until it cycles smoothly and rhythmically.

Focus on your breath. Inhale as sexual energy rises in your body, hold your breath briefly as the energy reaches the top of your head, and exhale as the energy moves back down your body.

Practice this exercise until you feel comfortable and confident cycling your sexual energy through your body.

Transmuting Your Sexual Energy

Once you have mastered the control of your sexual energy without releasing it through orgasm, you can redirect it into creative projects or actions, providing an energetic boost to endeavors such as workouts or business tasks.

This exercise is versatile and can be performed anywhere and at any time. You can initiate the exercise when you naturally feel arousal or intentionally cultivate inner arousal.

As you sense your sexual energy starting to rise, visualize it spreading throughout your entire body—flowing into your arms, legs, and up to the top of your head. Picture this energy moving through every cell of your body until you feel completely charged with it.

While taking action, feel this energy fueling whatever you're working on and envision it being infused into the task at hand.

For instance:

If you're painting, imagine this energy empowering your hand as the paintbrush touches the canvas.

If you're writing, visualize it coursing through your fingers and onto the keyboard.

If you're exercising, imagine your sexual energy building in the specific muscles you're working out, giving your lifts an added boost.

To enhance magnetism in a sales presentation, set the intention that this energy will radiate through you and captivate your audience.

Using Your Sexual Energy in Spellcasting

To direct your sexual energy to a specific goal, two highly effective methods involve channeling the energy into the spell without orgasmic release and charging a sigil with the power of your orgasm.

With the first method, prepare the magickal working you're undertaking, whether it's a simple demonic sigil charging, candle spell, or other type of spell you're doing such as a charm bag, poppet, or talisman.

Instead of channeling energy as you normally would into the working to charge it, perform the exercise 'conjuring up and harnessing your sexual energy' and then imagine that sexual energy running down through your arms, and out through your hands as you're holding the item associated with the spell you're doing.

As this energy is flowing, hold in your mind's eye a mental picture of the desired outcome you want to achieve from your spell.

With this method, you're not releasing the energy through orgasm. Instead, it's being intentionally moved from your body into the spell items you're working with as you're picturing the spell having worked successfully.

With the sigil method, you'll first create a symbol that represents your desired outcome based on a statement of intention.

To do this, think about a goal you'd like to manifest. With sigil work, I've found that smaller, very specific goals work best.

Let's say you want to manifest $25,000 per month in your business, but the most you've every made is $2000. You'll probably have more success reaching that goal if you create a sigil for 'sign a new client this month' or 'receive $3000 through my business' rather than jumping to creating a sigil for $25,000.

Once you're clear on your goal, write out a statement of intention. Using the above example, this could be: It is my will to sign a new client this month.

Before continuing, check in with your body and see how true your goal feels for you. Do you believe you can sign on a new client this month or are you feeling resistance around it?

Refer to the mindset section of the book under Manifesting Your Will to shift any beliefs you might be holding that can interfere with your magick. Rewrite your goal to make it more believable if necessary.

When you have your clear statement of intent written on a piece of paper, cross out all of the vowels and the repeating consonants so you're left with a small handle of letters.

Using the statement 'It is my will to sign a new client this month', you'll be left with the letters TSMWLGNCH

From here, take the letters and create a symbol out of them.

You can do this by layering the letters on top of each other, joining them together any way you like, or doing both until you're satisfied with the outcome. Play around with the design, simplifying it or adding more lines and shapes to it until it feels complete to you.

I've intentionally left out images of what a completed sigil should look like because this is an intuitively guided process.

You'll know exactly how to take the letters of your statement of intent and create a unique image that will speak directly to your subconscious mind, which is the basis of sigil magick.

With a sigil, you're creating a symbolic representation of your desires that's imprinted with the energy of your goal but without using the language of the conscious mind.

When you have a sigil design you're pleased with, re-draw it on a blank piece of paper. I find sigils that are a few inches in size are the easiest to work with but you may prefer to make yours smaller or larger.

To charge your sigil with sexual energy, you can cast a demonic circle and do the working at your altar, or the magick can be performed in bed or wherever is comfortable for you.

Begin by arousing your sexual energy through solo masturbation or with the help of a partner(s).

Feel this sexual energy circulating through your body, using your breath to control the speed that the energy is moving and to help build it up to its full potency.

When you feel yourself getting close to orgasm, gaze at your sigil and clear your mind. Focus only on the sigil as you release into orgasm.

Trust that your desired outcome, that was coded into the sigil itself has clearly been sent out the Universe.

When you're finished, you can burn the sigil, rip up the paper and toss it in the trash, or keep it to continue working with it in other forms of spellwork.

If you are continuing to use the sigil, keep in mind that the magick has already worked. Your order has already been placed with the Universe. Any additional spells you do with the sigil will be to charge the successful working with even more power.

Using Sexual Fluids in Your Magick

Given that sexual fluids contain the essence of life force energy, they can be used to enhance magickal workings associated with growth and increase.

Sexual fluids can be used to anoint a sigil if you're continuing to work with it after it's been charged as outlined above. You can also use fluids to anoint candles, poppets, charm bags, or add a few drops to ritual oils you're using.

If you're collecting fluids for later use, they can be stored in a small plastic container in the freezer. When you're ready to use them, you can either defrost the entire amount or chip off a small portion of the frozen material.

Chapter 15: Blood Magick

For a lot of people, working with blood in magick conjures up gruesome images of animal sacrifice, or the dramatic slashing of hands with blood spilling into chalices or onto sigils. This is not what we're doing here.

While animal sacrifice is part of some magickal systems, it's not part of Luciferianism, and the amount of blood used in ritual is a single drop or two.

When working with blood, just like with other bodily fluids, safety has to be taken into account. If you're working with other people in your practice, be aware that many diseases can be spread through the sharing of fluids and you'll need to take precautions to ensure that doesn't happen.

Whether you're working alone, or with other consenting adults, the harvesting of blood should be done with a new, clean diabetic lancet. This will ensure you're using a sterile tool, and since just a quick prick of the finger is required to get a drop of blood, you're not going to cause any harm to yourself or others.

I'll add here that blood magick is not an essential practice in Luciferianism or Demonolotry. If you don't feel drawn to incorporate it into your work, that's perfectly ok. Tune into your intuition and go with your gut.

If you're feeling drawn to it but experiencing a bit of hesitation, do some journaling around the reservations you're feeling. You might find that blood magick is a part of your path, helping you break through fear, or you might find that it's really not meant for you.

If it's just the letting of fresh blood through finger pricking that you don't like, but you still want to incorporate blood into your magick, period blood can be collected and used.

The Mechanics of Blood Magick

Our blood carries in it our vital essence. It contains our life force energy, as we need it for survival, and it's deeply unique to us as our blood is coded with the energy of our very beingness.

When we're working with blood in magick, we're channeling this life force energy, through the vessel of the blood, into any type of spell we're doing. We're putting our very life into the working.

Even though we're using a single drop of blood when doing this, the power behind it is immense and it forces us to break through taboos and fear.

To use blood in your ritual workings, have a clear idea of why you're using it to begin with.

Do you want to offer a drop on a demonic sigil to connect you to the outcome of a spell you're doing with that demon?

Is it being used as an offering to a demon?

Are going to add a drop to a magickal oil you're making?

Will it be used to anoint a candle, charm bag, or other ritual tool?

Are you going to combine blood magick with sex magick and spill a drop as you release into orgasm?

How to Use Blood in Spellcasting

With your diabetic lancet in hand, think about the purpose of the magickal work you're doing.

Then visualize your goal as you build up your energy. You are coding your blood with the frequency of your desired outcome and that frequency will be channeled into your spell.

Take your time with this exercise, getting all of your senses involved as you focus on the outcome you want to achieve.

Let's say you're doing a spell to manifest a vacation to the beach.

See yourself sitting in the sand overlooking the ocean as the seagulls circle overhead.

Hear the sound of the birds squawking, the laughter of the people around you, and the water lapping up against the shore.

Smell the salty sea air and sunscreen on your body.

Taste the sweetness of the tropical drink you're sipping on and the sensation in your mouth and throat as the icy cold liquid hits.

Go there in your mind and body and fully immerse yourself in the experience as much as possible. Once you're feeling the energy of the experience in your body, amplify it. Pretend you're turning up the dial on the experience to its highest setting until your body is buzzing with the frequency of your manifestation.

When you reach the point where you can't imagine the feeling being able to get any stronger, take your diabetic lancet and lightly prick your thumb or a finger.

Release the blood onto the magickal item you're working with knowing that you've just powerfully imprinted the item with your life essence that's been coded with the exact frequency of your goal.

Chapter 16: The Blood Baptism

This baptism was shown to me by Belial after doing some deep inner work and reflection on releasing myself from the past.

I had been feeling disconnected from my purpose and vision. Even though I had clarity on the things I was manifesting in my life and business, I was having a hard time connecting to the frequency of that vision.

The moment I completed the baptism, I felt closer to Lucifer and the demonic, and grounded into the new reality I was creating. It felt like I'd woken up in the life I'd been trying to live, and was now fully present in it.

Use this ritual as a statement of your commitment to the Luciferian path, or any time you feel like you need to release yourself from the past in order to move confidently into your future. New moons, as well as your birthday, are also great times to do this.

To begin, cast a demonic circle and go to your astral temple space.

Once there, call on Lucifer and Belial to join you.

Ask Lucifer to help you see anything that's preventing you from manifesting your goals, or advancing on your spiritual path.

Have him illuminate anything in the shadows that needs to be brought forth and ask him to help you see anything that you need see from a different perspective.

If you need time to do some journaling on these things so you have a deeper understanding of them, or if you feel you need time to process anything emotionally, do so before moving forward with the baptism.

Visualize Lucifer standing on one side of you and Belial on the other, and imagine a large pool of blood a few feet in front of you.

Imagine walking over to this pool while Lucifer and Belial walk along beside you. As you stand at the edge of the pool, say aloud **'I now release myself from the past and move confidently into my future knowing that I am always divinely guided, supported, and protected by the demonic realm.'**

See yourself walking down the steps of the pool, with Lucifer and Belial still beside you, until you're up to your chest in blood.

Visualize Lucifer and Belial tipping you back into the blood until you're fully submerged, and then lifting you back upright.

If you've ever witnessed or taken part in a Christian baptism, you'll find these actions to be very familiar. With this blood baptism, however, you are not submitting to the demonic. You are symbolically releasing anything from the past that's hindering your growth with their support.

As you walk out of the pool, see a throne waiting for you a feet away. Claim it. This is your rightful place to rule your life from.

As you sit on the throne, feel your personal power surging through you. You've just stepped into a whole new era. You are the Queen/King of your life and ruler of your destiny.

Finally, call upon Belial to help you ground into this new level of personal power and responsibility.

Are there any new habits you need to form?

Are there systems and structures you need to put into place to support your goals?

What actions are you being guided to take today as the ruler of your reality?

To complete the blood baptism ritual, thank Lucifer and Belial for their presence and have them exit your astral temple space.

If there's any other magickal working you feel called to do, complete it and when you're ready, leave your temple space and come fully back into the physical realm.

Conclusion

You are the magick you've been seeking in your life.

You are the ultimate spell.

You hold everything you desire within.

Lucifer and the demonic can help you see that, and I hope that will be your experience after reading this book.

About the Author

Kelly Dawn is a Witch, Psychic Guide, and Spiritual Mentor. She's been practicing witchcraft off and on since her early teens and since 2016 has worked primarily as a Demonolatress after a powerful encounter with Lucifer.

Through her work as a Psychic Guide and Coach, she is known as the entrepreneurs' secret weapon, helping visionaries and leaders shift their mindset and energy so they become magnetic to their desires, making their next-level life and business dreams a reality.

In her role as a Spiritual Mentor, she helps those who are drawn to the path of witchcraft work with the unseen realm, develop their psychic abilities, and fully embody their most empowered selves through the use of magick and ritual, enabling them to create tangible results in their lives.

To learn more, visit www.kellydawn.co

Made in United States
Troutdale, OR
07/13/2024

21209737R00105